PENNSYLVANIA'S HISTORIC RESTAURANTS

and their recipes

JOHN F. BLAIR, *Publisher*
Winston-Salem, North Carolina

PENNSYLVANIA'S HISTORIC RESTAURANTS

and their recipes

by DAWN O'BRIEN
and CLAIRE WALTER

Drawings by Patsy Faires

Book design by Virginia Ingram
Drawings by Patsy Faires
Cover Photographs by Bernard Carpenter
Composition by Superior Typesetters, Inc.
Manufactured by Donnelley Printing Company

Library of Congress Cataloging-in-Publication Data

O'Brien, Dawn
Pennsylvania's historic restaurants and their recipes.

Includes index.
1. Cookery—Pennsylvania. 2. Restaurants, lunch
rooms, etc.—Pennsylvania—Directories. 3. Historic
buildings—Pennsylvania. I. Walter, Claire. II. Title.
TX715.0'286 1986   641.5'09748   86-3593
ISBN 0-89587-046-0

DEDICATION

When my husband, John O'Brien, is piqued, his jaw tightens. Extreme anger causes his mouth to draw to a thin white line, while his eyes narrow to slits and pulsate like Charles Manson's. The day he was detained in a New Jersey airport with a snapping turtle for snapper soup in tow, he wore the latter expression. Although the huge turtle was wrapped in an armor of aluminum wrap, its skeleton was detected through the airport's x-ray machine.

Airport security officials seemed to materialize out of the cement block walls. Suspecting that some deviant was attempting to transport human remains, they demanded that John unwrap the bundle. Here John's piqued expression changed to its livid stage. He tersely told them, "Unwrap it yourself!" Afraid his next line would be Clint Eastwood's "Go ahead, make my day," security obliged. When the turtle's little tail and feet jutted out, security returned it to John. A small altercation ensued as to exactly who would rewrap the turtle. Security lost.

John has grown increasingly supportive with each book, and since I fear the "turtle caper" may thwart future support altogether, I dedicate my part of this book to my handsome, clever, suave and sophisticated husband, John J. O' Brien.

Dawn O'Brien

To my son Andrew Cameron-Walter, a toddler while this book was in preparation, who went straight from Pablum to pâté.

Claire Walter

CONTENTS

x

ACKNOWLEDGMENTS

Pennsylvania was a fun state to research, offering so many wonderful historic restaurants that it would take at least three books to tell her whole story. But to the many and varied people who aided us, especially those at the fifty restaurants who shared their stories, food and recipes with us, we are indebted and thankful. There were also those who went out of their way to be helpful. A special thank you to the following:

To: Sally Moore, past publicity director of the Pennsylvania Bureau of Travel Development, to whom we owe the greatest debt of thanks.

To: The Pennsylvania chambers of commerce, county tourist promotion agencies, city travel bureaus, especially to Karen Afflerbach, Kim Derderian, Betty Dudenhaver, Rhonda Gemelli, Norene Lahr, Chuck Leonard, Phil Magaldi, Michelle E. Mancini, Pat Redmond, Fred E. Ruppenthal, Anne Stewart, Stephanie Swatkowski, Laurie Ward, Chrissy White and Cindi Young.

To: David Shipley of USAir, who helped us get to the far corners of Pennsylvania.

To: The chefs who shared their time and talent with us.

To: The restaurateurs, who shared wonderful histories.

To: The artist, Patsy Faires, who did such a beautiful job on the artwork for the restaurants of Virginia that we asked her to do the same for Pennsylvania.

To: Our editor, Virginia Hege, for understanding.

To: Our art director, Virginia Ingram, for her skill in making each book in this series a visual winner.

To: Shirley Gustafson, Saxton Powell and Marcia Sullivan for their accuracy and aid in testing recipes.

To: Dr. David Burns, whose book *Feeling Good* gave the courage that lead to the inspiration for this series.

To: A diverse flock of guinea pigs who vow that each state's restaurants are better than the last.

PREFACE

Some people tell me that they read cookbooks like novels, which lights up my day. Others have said that a cookbook is better than a sleeping pill, which does not light up my day. Then they quickly add, "You know, half a cup of flour, half a cup of sugar, 2 eggs, etc. . . ." Reading page after page of ingredients just seems to have a hypnotizing effect. To those people I always suggest that they read the story of each restaurant to keep them awake. Initially (four cookbooks ago), it was discovering the unique stories in each historic restaurant that woke me up to writing restaurant guide–cookbooks.

My first two books were written solo, but with four more in the hopper it became clear that there was too much traveling, writing and testing of recipes to be done by one person. I needed collaborators with similar qualifications and interests. Ah, but where to find this special breed?

When people discover my vocation they believe that I've invented the dream job of all time, and in theory they are right. When I'm on the road, waking up each morning is like Christmas. First, you drive up to a historical restaurant, which for me is like shaking the box to see what is inside; then, unearthing the story that lies in the structure's past is akin to unwrapping the package. This usually occurs while sampling new or unusually prepared dishes. Sounds good, doesn't it? Well, there are many writers all too willing to tackle that part of the job. However, their enthusiasm wains when they discover the other integral factors involved in bringing these stories and recipes to print. Just finding those restaurants is a tedious process that is first begun with each state's department of commerce.

Before I called Pennsylvania's Travel Bureau, I did not know that the state motto was "You've got a friend in Pennsylvania," but the first telephone call made me realize that this was a motto not based on catchy rhetoric. I was soon to find out how true the slogan actually is.

The former publicity director of the Pennsylvania Bureau of Development, Sally Moore, was my first contact, and that initial introduction was one of enthusiasm, cooperation, efficiency and friendship. I explained my two major needs: a collaborator, and information on how to find Pennsylvania's historic restaurants. Never did I expect to accomplish both in one phone call, but thanks to Sally's understanding of my project, Pennsylvania's door of friendship was opened.

I explained that the restaurant itself did not have to be historic, but the building in which the restaurant is housed must be at least fifty years old, or it must be a reconstructed building on a significant historic site (in accordance with the criteria used by the National Register when designating a structure, site or district as historic). My criteria are not quite as stringent as the National Register's, which include a mountain of other qualifications, but in essence we are in agreement on the definition of what constitutes a historic building.

Sally Moore dispatched a letter to Pennsylvania's county tourist promotion agencies, asking them to help me seek out their historic restaurants. And I was given a list of travel collaborators who were also gourmet cooks. After many interesting phone calls and exchange of portfolios, I arranged to collaborate with Claire Walter.

The overwhelming positive response from Pennsylvania's county tourist promotion agencies gave me far more than I had bargained for. It took weeks of whittling the qualified restaurants down to a mere fifty, which is the number allowed for each book in the cookbook series. Claire was anxious to get started, so she interviewed a number of restaurants before we met. Then, the county tourist promotion agencies not only helped me set up appointments, but they cheerfully chauffeured me to them as well. I finally met Claire, and we hit the snowy trail, sometimes visiting the restaurant together and sometimes splitting up when there were dual appointments. With the exception of one icy day when highways were closed, we covered about half of our goal. Then I went home to prepare for the exploration of Maryland, while Claire continued to seek out the restaurants that were selected.

What a difference it makes when an entire state treats your project with eagerness! Without question, Claire and I received such treatment from tourism directors, restaurateurs and chefs throughout the state. For us, Pennsylvania has truly become a symbol of friendship.

Erie

Meadville
•
• Conneaut Lake
•
Waterford

Coraopolis-Moon Township
•
 Pittsburgh

• Scenery Hill

Scranton

Ballietsville ●

Allentown ●   ● Bethlehem
Mertztown ●   ● Limeport
Quakertown ●   ● Lumberville

Lebanon   Myerstown
Annville ●   ●   ● Reading   Doylestown ●
Hershey ●

Middletown ●   Coventryville ●   ● Gwnedd
Mount Joy   Lionville   Norristown ●
Wrightstown ●   ● Lancaster   Exton   Merion ●
West Chester ●   Philadelphia
Thornton ●   ● Dilworthtown
Abbottstown   West Grove ●
Gettysburg

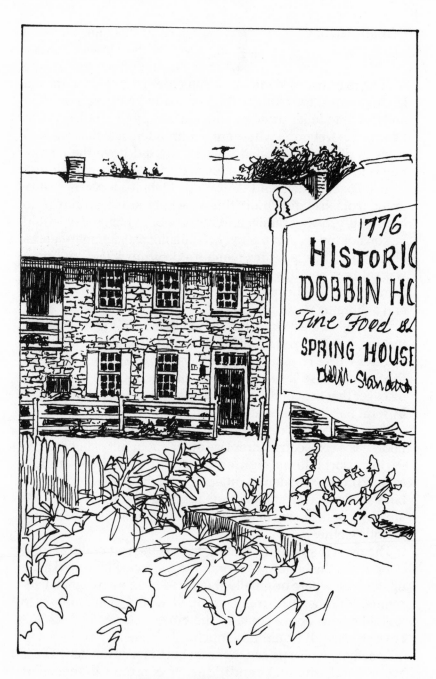

DOBBIN HOUSE
Gettysburg

DOBBIN HOUSE It was hard to dislodge me from the foyer of the Dobbin House. While Dawn O'Brien and I were waiting to be ushered into the dining room, I inspected the old kitchen wares, the corner cupboard loaded with old porcelain and the chandelier studded with hand-dipped candles. It was Dawn, the veteran, who gently reminded me that we had work to do—and I'm glad I eventually did leave the memorabilia to eat at this restaurant in Gettysburg's oldest building.

In 1776, the Reverend Alexander Dobbin, a recent immigrant from Ireland, built this spacious stone structure to house his growing family and his school, which today would be considered a combination of a theological seminary and a liberal arts college. After Dobbin's death in 1809, the house was sold at a sheriff's sale. In the years that followed, it was in turn a Civil War hospital, an apartment building, a museum and a diorama.

In 1976, Jackie White purchased the building and began turning it into a restaurant. She found a nineteen-foot-long counter with a chestnut base and walnut top, a perfect bar for the Springhouse Tavern in the basement. She was stunned to discover that the counter had been in the general store owned by John Baish—her great-grandfather.

The Library, one of several small dining rooms on the main floor, has a cozy corner fireplace and a room full of books. The Parlor sports some eighteenth-century graffiti—initials carved on the wooden mantlepiece, perhaps by one of Dobbin's students. Upstairs is the Spinning Room, whose walls are hung with skeins of flax and cotton, spinning wheels and antique clothes.

The most inspired decorating trick is the rest of the second floor. From the building's diorama days, Jackie inherited a big open space where originally there had been many small bedrooms. She installed frames draped with Colonial fabric to look like beds above some of the tables. These "bed-tables" are a creative and charming touch.

Creativity is also prized in the Dobbin House kitchen. There are several unusual renditions of common dishes. For

2

instance, the Baked King's Onion Soup has satisfying chunks of meat, a lacing of sherry and a topping of two cheeses. The fine Roast Duck Adams County is cooked with apple, orange and lime.

I don't know how anyone, even a dieter, can resist dipping into the breadbasket for Banana-Coconut, Blueberry or Pear Bread. But the damage can be minimized with one of several salads (including fresh fruit), a broiled Seafarer's Feast (flounder, shrimp, scallops and crabmeat) or Broiled Alaskan King Crab Legs.—c.w.

The Dobbin House is located at 89 Steinwehr Avenue in Gettysburg. Lunch is served daily from 11:30 a.m. until 1:00 p.m. Dinner is served from 5:00 p.m. until 9:00 p.m., Monday through Thursday, and from 5:00 p.m. until 10:00 p.m., Friday and Saturday. Sunday brunch is served from 11:30 a.m. until 2:00 p.m., April through December. For reservations (suggested) call (717) 334-2100.

DOBBIN HOUSE'S ROAST DUCK ADAMS COUNTY

1 4- to 5-pound duck	1 lime, cut into 4 wedges
3 cups apple cider	and then sliced ¼ inch
⅛ teaspoon ginger	thick
⅛ teaspoon nutmeg	2 tablespoons brown sugar
1 orange, cut into 6 wedges	2 tablespoons applejack
and then sliced ¼ inch	1 tablespoon cornstarch
thick	2 apples, cut into wedges

Preheat oven to 375 degrees. Halve duck by cutting through the breastbone and along both sides of the backbone. Also remove the large flap of neck skin and cut the wings at the first joint. Rinse the duck halves under cold water and place, skin side up, in a 2-inch-deep baking dish. Pour cider over duck and sprinkle with ginger and nutmeg. Place one-fourth of the orange pieces and one-fourth of the lime pieces over the duck. Cover pan with foil and bake for 2 hours or until the leg wiggles easily. Remove the roasting pan from the oven and raise the temperature to 425 degrees.

3

Remove duck to a platter and keep warm. Pour pan juices into a small saucepan and skim the grease from the top. Add brown sugar and applejack and bring to a boil. Dissolve cornstarch in ¼ cup cold water and stir into the boiling juices. Continue stirring until sauce is thickened.

Place remaining orange and lime slices into another small saucepan with enough cold water to cover. Bring to a boil and then drain off water. Add the citrus fruit to the sauce and keep warm. Place apple wedges on a cookie sheet and top with duck halves. Bake for 10 minutes until apple slices are hot and duck skin is crisp. Place duck on a serving platter and top with warm sauce. Serves 2 to 4.

DOBBIN HOUSE'S BAKED KING'S ONION SOUP

6 cups beef stock
2 tablespoons sweet butter
6 medium onions, peeled and diced
1 cup stewing beef, cut into ½-inch cubes

1 cup dry sherry
6 slices good-quality white bread
12 slices Swiss cheese
12 slices Provolone cheese

Bring beef stock to a slow boil in a large saucepan. In a skillet, melt butter and sauté onions until they begin to yellow. Meanwhile, brown beef in another skillet. Add onions, beef and sherry to the stock and simmer for 30 minutes. When ready to serve, fill six ovenproof bowls with soup. Place 1 slice of bread, 2 slices of Swiss cheese and 2 slices of Provolone (in that order) on top of each serving. Place under broiler until cheese browns. Serves 6.

FARNSWORTH HOUSE
Gettysburg

FARNSWORTH HOUSE It isn't difficult to persuade Loring H. Shultz, owner of the Farnsworth House, to show you the attic of his restaurant. There, during the epic Civil War battle at Gettysburg, Confederate sharpshooters lay prone at a small, low window to pick off enemy traffic on Baltimore Hill. One of them, it is believed, accidentally shot Jennie Wade in her house at the bottom of the hill; she was Gettysburg's only civilian death.

Shultz does a great show-and-tell routine in that attic, hauling out memorabilia and telling grand stories about the battle. At the Farnsworth House, you may hold a Civil War pistol, peer through a pair of antique eyeglasses or finger the cloth of an old uniform. Much of the collection could be in a museum, but no museum would so freely let visitors handle the wares.

The oldest part of the house, dating to 1810, is the low-ceilinged Lee Room. The adjacent Meade Room is in an addition that was put onto the front of the original house thirteen years later. Its graceful brick facade is what we see today from Baltimore Street.

In the Meade Room, dominated by an oil portrait of the Union general, are shelved 110 volumes of a complete Civil War history published around 1900 by the U.S. Government. Framed and hanging on the wall is the letter in which George Pickett accepted a commission as a captain in the Confederate Army.

Tourists flock here both for the atmosphere and for the reasonably priced entrées, sandwiches and salads available throughout the day and evening. A more ambitious dinner menu is offered in the evening only.

I tasted both the Goober Pea Soup, a smooth, peanutty brew, and the hearty Ham and Bean Soup. Popular entrées include Colonial Game Pie (a stick-to-the-ribs combo of pheasant, duck and turkey under an egg-pastry mantle) and the seafood offering, A Made Dish of Shrimp & Lobster, a whimsical old term for what we would today call a casserole. Desserts include rich Rum Cream Pie, moist Walnut Apple Cake that is topped with nutmeg sauce and Black Walnut Ice Cream.

Dieters might select a Plate of Old Cheddar Cheese, Crackers and Fresh Apple as a starter, and perhaps Baked Fillet of Flounder or the half-pound Chopped Sirloin as a main course. Zucchini and Tomato is a low-calorie side dish.

Mamie Eisenhower, widow of former president Dwight Eisenhower, was often a guest at the Farnsworth House after the restaurant opened in 1972, for Ike's farm is not far away. She was partial to the flounder, and she always ordered a Hot Fudge Sundae for dessert. Another prominent guest was Michael Shaara, author of *The Killer Angels*, the Pulitzer Prize-winning novel about the Battle of Gettysburg. Loring Shultz doesn't remember what Shaara ate; they were too busy swapping Civil War stories.—c.w.

The Farnsworth House is located at 401 Baltimore Street in Gettysburg. A light menu, suitable for luncheon or supper, is served from 11:00 a.m. until 10:00 p.m., seven days a week. The dinner menu is served from 5:00 p.m. until 10:00 p.m., nightly. For reservations (requested) call (717) 334-8838.

FARNSWORTH HOUSE'S A MADE DISH OF SHRIMP & LOBSTER

1¼ sticks margarine	1 cup cooked baby shrimp, peeled
2 green peppers, seeded and diced	1¼ ounces dry cocktail sherry
2 medium onions, diced	1 teaspoon Worcestershire sauce
¼ pound wild rice	
½ pound long grain rice	1 teaspoon lemon juice
1 quart boiling water	1 tablespoon salt (or to taste)
4 cups crushed tomatoes (2 16-ounce cans)	¼ teaspoon white pepper
½ cup canned mushrooms, drained	1½ pounds cooked lobster meat, chopped

Melt margarine in a saucepan. Sauté green pepper and onion until wilted. Stir in wild and long grain rice. Add boiling water and cook over low heat until rice is tender, about 30 minutes. Meanwhile, in a large bowl mix the tomatoes, mush-

7

rooms, shrimp, sherry, Worcestershire sauce, lemon juice, salt and pepper. Add cooked rice and vegetable mixture and mix well. Add lobster meat and mix well. Serves 12.

FARNSWORTH HOUSE'S RUM CREAM PIE

¼ ounce unflavored gelatin
¾ cup cold tap water
4 egg yolks
½ cup sugar
1½ ounces rum
1 pint heavy whipping
  cream

1 9-inch graham cracker
  crust (see index)
1 square unsweetened
  chocolate

Soften gelatin in cold water, heat over low heat until dissolved and set aside to cool to lukewarm. In a mixing bowl, beat egg yolks and sugar until light and fluffy. Stir gelatin, then rum into egg mixture, mixing well. Place in refrigerator. Whip cream until it stands in soft peaks. Fold whipped cream and egg mixture together. Spoon into pie crust and refrigerate. Garnish with unsweetened chocolate, grated or shredded over the top. Yields 1 pie.

FARNSWORTH HOUSE'S HAM AND BEAN SOUP

6 cups water
½ pound Great Northern
  beans, soaked overnight
  in cold water
2 teaspoons salt

1 small onion, chopped
pinch of white pepper
1 teaspoon parsley flakes
2 ounces chopped ham

Place all ingredients in a large saucepan. Bring to a boil, then lower the heat, cover and simmer until beans are soft, about 2 to 4 hours. Serves 8.

THE ALTLAND HOUSE
Abbottstown

THE ALTLAND HOUSE **P**eople often ask what spurs me to write about historic restaurants. Not until I visited The Altland House did the real answer emerge for me. Betty Haugh, the restaurant's owner, was explaining how, since 1750, The Altland House had been "a place where tired and dusty people and horses could find a place to eat, drink, and rest." Horses! Betty's reference to the livery stable triggered my memory. When I was a child, my Grandmother Lee often told me fascinating stories of the days when she helped her parents run their hotel and livery stable. Those stories piqued my early curiosity about history, a curiosity that obviously has never been satiated. So, when I saw this venerable old Victorian restaurant standing as a monument to the solid structural sense of early craftsmen, I had to know its story.

Inside, an eighteen-foot mural shows Abbottstown Square as it looked in 1880, when Reuben Altland purchased this "public house of entertainment." Sure enough, that mural shows a scene—with horses—very much like those my grandmother used to create for me.

Betty Haugh began working at The Altland House at age thirteen. Those were the days of the Great Depression, and times were so hard that the entire menu consisted of chicken and waffles. Today's guests would never associate those meager offerings with the imaginative treats now served at the restaurant.

My dinner companion, Laurie Ward, and I were first invited to sample a tray of hot hors d'oeuvres. Such appetizers may be accompanied by what The Altland House calls their 100 Per Cent Martini, or by a French '75, a fabulous champagne and gin combination. Laurie was pleased with a dry yet fruity York White Rosé from the local Naylor Vineyard.

We both adored the Stuffed Artichoke Bottoms with Crabmeat and Hollandaise, but I especially enjoyed their exceptional Turtle Soup. (Unfortunately for home cooks, the recipe is the late Mr. Tom Haugh's creation and a well-guarded secret, so I couldn't add it to the recipe section.) Next, a regional warm Sweet and Sour Bacon Dressing on a Bibb Lettuce Salad was a perfect, piquant introduction to their famed Baked Imperial Crab.

At too many restaurants, vegetables are treated as an afterthought, but not at The Altland House. Before my meal here, beets had not been on my list of preferred vegetables, but a taste of Harvard Beets and Pineapple changed my mind. Corn pudding is always a favorite, and theirs was no exception.

Laurie told me that The Altland House was one of President Eisenhower's special places to bring friends. I wonder if that had anything to do with the Chocolate Mousse Pie they served for dessert. That temptation alone would certainly prompt my return visit.

The Altland House is located at the intersection of routes 30 and 194 in Abbottstown. Meals are served from 11:00 a.m. until 10:00 p.m., Tuesday through Thursday, and from 11:00 a.m. until 11:00 p.m. on Friday and Saturday. Sunday dinner is served from noon until 8:00 p.m. For reservations (preferred) call (717) 259-9535.

THE ALTLAND HOUSE'S CHOCOLATE MOUSSE PIE

1 9-inch graham cracker pie crust (see index)
1 6-ounce package semi-sweet chocolate chips
1 8-ounce package cream cheese, softened
9 tablespoons plus 1 teaspoon brown sugar
1 tablespoon powdered instant coffee or freeze-dried coffee
⅛ teaspoon salt
1 teaspoon vanilla
2 eggs, separated
2 cups whipping cream
½ ounce grated chocolate

Bake pie shell according to recipe directions. In a double boiler, heat chocolate chips until melted; cool 10 minutes. With an electric mixer on low speed, beat cream cheese with 5 tablespoons plus 1 teaspoon brown sugar, the coffee, salt and vanilla until smooth. Add egg yolks and melted chocolate, beating until smooth. In a separate, chilled bowl (glass or stainless steel give best results) beat egg whites on high until stiff peaks form. Beat in 4 tablespoons brown sugar until stiff

11

peaks form again. Fold egg whites into chocolate mixture. Whip cream; reserve ½ cup, and fold remaining whipped cream into chocolate mixture. Pour mixture into pie shell. Mound reserved whipped cream on top. Garnish with grated chocolate if desired. Cover; freeze at least 8 hours. Remove from freezer 20 minutes before serving. Yields 1 pie.

THE ALTLAND HOUSE'S HARVARD BEETS AND PINEAPPLE

1 pound can whole baby
  beets with juice
1 8½-ounce can pineapple
  chunks in heavy syrup
2½ ounces pineapple juice
2 tablespoons plus 1
  teaspoon sugar

½ tablespoon white vinegar
½ teaspoon salt
dash of white pepper
1 tablespoon cornstarch
¼ cup water

Place the beets with juice, pineapple chunks and pineapple juice in a saucepan and bring to a boil. Add the sugar, vinegar, salt and pepper. In a separate pan, dissolve the cornstarch in the water and blend into beet mixture. Bring to a boil, stirring occasionally. Reduce heat and simmer for about 5 to 8 minutes. Serves 4 to 6.

THE ALTLAND HOUSE'S CORN PUDDING

3½ tablespoons flour
3½ tablespoons sugar
dash of salt
dash of white pepper
2 eggs, well beaten

1 pound can cream-style
  corn
½ cup plus 2 tablespoons
  milk

Mix dry ingredients together; stir in beaten eggs, corn and milk. Pour into a greased 8-inch square pan (or one of equivalent size). Place pan into a larger pan containing about 1 inch of hot water. Bake at 275 degrees for 1 hour or until set. Serves 4 to 6.

RED ROSE INN
West Grove

RED ROSE INN The Young Lady who lives on the third floor doesn't approve of wine. Indian Joe inhabits the cellar and once scared the daylights out of the dog. These are the ghosts of the Red Rose Inn.

Indian Joe, the basement spirit, is reputedly the ghost of an eighteenth-century man. As the tale goes, a group of fur traders killed him in retribution for some transgression now lost to history. They murdered the wrong man, however, and to hide the deed, they buried him in the cellar walls.

Former owner John Bussey first encountered Indian Joe one evening in 1978 while making the rounds of the inn. While in the basement, he was startled by a shadow, apparently without a source. Bussey's dog was terrified. Her hair stood on end, and she refused to go into the cellar again as long as she lived.

Little is known about the other spirit, simply called the Young Lady, except that she too met an unexpected death. She first made her presence known to the Busseys when they were taking some friends on a tour of the building. On the third floor, a wine glass Mary Ann Bussey was carrying was taken from her hand and smashed. The group beat a hasty retreat. When the Busseys went upstairs the following day, the glass had been swept up.

On another occasion, a wine encyclopedia was pulled off a bookshelf and thrown aside. Chairs have been moved several times from the wall to a window. Who can guess what the Young Lady is watching for?

I saw no ghosts at the Red Rose Inn—merely the specter of course after course of fine food flitting across the table. When I visited, the menu featured American dishes, both traditional and adapted: Stuffed Baked Flounder or Stuffed Rainbow Trout, Surf and Turf, various steak cuts, assorted poultry and several seafoods. Individual Beef Wellington, a tender fillet wrapped in a mantle of flaky pastry, was also offered.

Red Rose Inn has stood for nearly two and a half centuries on property deeded by William Penn. The oldest part, the 1740 Room, was originally a country store and inn along the Philadelphia–Baltimore Pike. Penn's deed calls for an unusual rent. To this day, one red rose is still presented to a direct descendant of William Penn on the first Saturday after Labor Day, locally known as Red Rose Rent Day. It has become traditional for neighborhood and visiting rose growers to exhibit prize blooms on that day.

Richard and Lee Covatta, who now own Red Rose Inn, have recently modified the menu to include Italian cuisine, as well as pheasant and duck.—c.w.

Red Rose Inn is located on Route 796 in West Grove. Lunch is served from 11:30 a.m. until 4:00 p.m., Monday through Saturday. Dinner is served from 4:00 p.m. until 9:00 p.m., Monday through Thursday; from 4:00 p.m. until 10:00 p.m. Friday and Saturday; and from 4:00 p.m. until 8:00 p.m. on Sunday. A Sunday brunch is served from 11:00 a.m. until 2:00 p.m. For reservations (required on weekends) call (215) 869-3003.

RED ROSE INN'S OYSTERS AU PERNOD WITH MUSHROOMS

10 fresh mushrooms	2 tablespoons butter
1 tablespoon sweet butter	dash of cayenne pepper
juice of 1 lemon	1 quart heavy cream
½ cup Pernod	3 dozen oysters, shucked

Remove stems from mushrooms and reserve for soup or another use. Cut caps into julienne strips. Sauté in 1 tablespoon sweet butter with lemon juice until liquid has cooked out from mushrooms. Strain and reserve this mushroom stock; set mushrooms aside. In a saucepan, combine Pernod and mushroom stock. Bring to boil and reduce to one-quarter of original volume. Remove from heat. Immediately stir in butter and cayenne and continue stirring until cooled. When liquid has cooled to lukewarm, stir in heavy cream. Return to heat and reduce to one-half original volume (consistency of cream sauce), stirring every 4 to 5 minutes to prevent burning or separating. Add julienned mushrooms. Spread 6 oysters in each of 6 individual casseroles. Spoon sauce over oysters and heat in a 400-degree oven for 10 minutes. Serves 6.

RED ROSE INN'S DUCK & MUSHROOM SALAD WITH HONEY-MUSTARD VINAIGRETTE

2 4- to 5-pound ducks	24 fresh mushrooms
Honey-Mustard Vinaigrette	8 ounces fresh spinach
(recipe below)	1 cup fancy pecan pieces

Roast ducks in a 350-degree oven for 1½ to 2 hours or until done. Remove from roasting pan and allow to cool. Remove breast and thigh meat from carcass, and cut meat into julienne strips. Marinate strips in Honey-Mustard Vinaigrette for 2 hours. Wipe mushrooms with a damp cloth, slice thinly and place in cold water until you are ready to serve. Wash spinach thoroughly and remove stems. Arrange marinated duck, mushrooms, spinach and pecan pieces on salad serving plate or individual salad plates. Serves 4 to 6.

Honey-Mustard Vinaigrette:

2 egg yolks	¼ cup Dijon mustard
¼ cup honey	½ cup cider vinegar
¼ cup brown sugar	2 cups salad oil
juice of 1 lemon	1 garlic clove, minced
1 teaspoon dry English	1 shallot bulb, minced
mustard	salt and pepper to taste

In a mixing bowl, combine egg yolks, honey, brown sugar, lemon juice, mustards and vinegar. Mix well. Slowly add oil in a thin, steady stream, whisking to give the vinaigrette body. Add garlic, shallot, salt and pepper. Cover and let stand in refrigerator one day before using.

DILWORTHTOWN INN
Dilworthtown

DILWORTHTOWN INN As you enter the foyer of the Dilworthtown Inn, you'll see on your right a painting depicting a colonial tavern. Look closely at the faces on two of the figures. The one on the far left belongs to current owner Timothy McCarthy, while the one on the right—the fellow with his arm in a sling—is the inn's manager, Jim Barnes. This touch of whimsy is a light stroke on the canvas of an elegant restaurant that is very serious about its food, its wines and its history.

That history stretches back to 1758, when James Dilworth built a house for his wife and eleven children. After James's death twelve years later, son Charles turned the family home into a tavern called The Sign of the Pennsylvania Farmer. Occupied by the British for five days during the Battle of Brandywine—the last shots of which were fired in Dilworthtown—the inn was ransacked by the English after the colonists were defeated. After the war, the tavern operated under various names until 1821, when it was first called the Dilworthtown Inn.

Today the original house and more recent additions contain eleven dining rooms on two floors, plus a charming lounge with a small bar and a working fireplace. One particularly enchanting dining room, once the Dilworth family's kitchen, is dominated by a nine-foot-wide fireplace and a restored beehive oven. Like the other dining rooms, it has just a few tables, providing an intimate atmosphere in a sizable restaurant.

Although the dining rooms are illuminated solely by gaslights and candles, the fine cuisine could even tolerate the spotlight's glare. To ease the dilemma of which hors d'oeuvre to select, ask for a sampling of several. My companion and I enjoyed perfect shrimp the size of a sumo wrestler's thumb, velvety Pâté de Volaille, chilled Fillet of Salmon and Smoked Bluefish.

Beef and seafood entrées prevail on the menu. I selected Crabe en Casserole. The Maryland lump crab was baked to perfection, but I must confess to feeling a twinge of envy

18

when a diner at the next table ordered the Filet de Boeuf au Poivre. This lusty filet mignon was glazed, flamed at the table and served with a sauce aromatic with green peppercorns.

If you are looking for an opportunity to splurge on Mouton-Rothschild or Château d'Yquem, the Dilworthtown Inn, with its extraordinary wine cellar, is the place. But for more modest budgets, the restaurant's private-label red and white Bordeaux are ideal.—c.w.

Dilworthtown Inn is located ¼ mile from Route 202 South in Dilworthtown, south of West Chester. Dinner is served from 5:30 p.m. until 10:30 p.m., Monday through Saturday, and from 3:00 p.m. until 9:00 p.m. on Sunday. For reservations (preferred) call (215) 399-1390.

DILWORTHTOWN INN'S PATE DE VOLAILLE

1 pound chicken breast meat
5 ounces chicken fat
½ pound pork fatback
7 shallots, minced and
  sautéed in butter
½ pound ice, crushed
2 teaspoons salt
1 teaspoon white pepper
1 teaspoon Worcestershire
  sauce
½ teaspoon Tabasco sauce
2 ounces ice, crushed
2 ounces carrots, cut into
  2-inch lengths
1 ounce celery, cut into
  2-inch lengths
1 pound sliced bacon

Dice chicken meat, chicken fat and fatback into 1-inch cubes. In a metal bowl that has been placed in a larger bowl of ice water, mix shallots, ½ pound of ice, salt and pepper with meats. When this mixture is thoroughly chilled, grind it through the ³⁄₁₆-inch die of a meat grinder into a metal bowl over ice. Chill mixture overnight. Grind again, using the ¹⁄₁₆-inch die of meat grinder. Chill. Stir in Worcestershire sauce and Tabasco sauce. In a food processor fitted with the steel chopping blade, chop mixture, adding 2 ounces of crushed ice. Blanch carrots and celery in boiling, salted water. Cool, then dice into ¼-inch cubes and add to meat mixture. Chill. Meanwhile, line a 12x4x4-inch pâté mold (or loaf pan of similar

19

size) with bacon slices, slightly overlapping slices and allowing enough to extend beyond the edge of the mold to fold back over the meat mixture. Tightly pack the mixture into the mold. Fold overhanging bacon over top of meat. Place a board or ovenproof pan over pâté to weight it down during cooking. Bake at 450 degrees until an internal temperature of 160 degrees is reached—approximately 45 minutes. Leave weight on pâté and cool on a wire rack until pâté reaches room temperature. Remove weight and refrigerate. Cut into ¼-inch slices to serve. Serves 10 to 15.

DILWORTHTOWN INN'S CRABE EN CASSEROLE

2 egg yolks
½ cup mayonnaise
1 teaspoon Dijon mustard
½ teaspoon Worcestershire
   sauce

dash of Tabasco sauce
¼ teaspoon salt (or to taste)
1 pound lump crabmeat,
   drained and picked over

Preheat oven to 425 degrees. Combine all ingredients except crabmeat, whisking together thoroughly. Gently fold in crabmeat, being careful not to break up chunks. Place mixture in a buttered casserole and bake until heated through and browned on top, approximately 10 minutes. Serves 2 to 3.

DILWORTHTOWN INN'S STUFFED TOMATOES

3 medium tomatoes
1 very small head of
   broccoli, cut into
   flowerets
1 small zucchini, washed

2 small or 1½ medium
   carrots, peeled
salt and pepper to taste
½ cup sour cream

Preheat oven to 350 degrees. Halve tomatoes horizontally and scoop out seeds, being careful to keep skin and pulp intact. In a food processor fitted with the chopping blade, combine broccoli, zucchini, carrots, salt and pepper and chop fine. Transfer mixture to a bowl and stir in sour cream. Stuff mixture into tomato halves. Place stuffed halves in a baking dish and bake about 15 to 20 minutes, until hot but not overcooked. Serves 6.

20

PACE ONE RESTAURANT
Thornton

PACE ONE RESTAURANT

During the American Revolution, colonial soldiers wounded at the Battle of the Brandywine were brought to the summer home of one George Gray, a prominent Whig. The women who cared for them became known as Gray Ladies, a name still used for hospital volunteers.

Since British muskets had a short firing range, many of the Americans were hit from the knees down. The Gray house hospital saw so many of these injuries that the crossroads at which it was located became known as Shintown.

The hamlet's name was changed to Thornton around 1830, when a general store was established on the Gray property, along with what is reputed to be the longest continually operating post office in the United States. It has changed very little since then, to this day remaining a quiet intersection with a couple of stores and a handful of houses.

Thornton's appeal was not lost on Ted Pace, a Pittsburgher who grew up in a family that ran every kind of restaurant from a luncheonette to a catering hall. He bought the old Gray property late in 1978 and opened a restaurant in the big stone barn where George Gray's horses were once stabled.

The young restaurateur has carved a very personal restaurant from the eighteenth-century barn. In a cozy dining room, the ceiling is supported by massive old beams. The subtle lighting comes from pierced tin fixtures, and the simple furniture is contemporary yet very much in keeping with the sturdy old barn. There is a large veranda with small-paned windows covering one entire wall. In summer, these windows are opened for *al fresco* dining.

The cuisine is one of the most creative I've encountered. The only way I can describe the fare, designed by Ted "to match the beams," is Country Imaginative. Many of the dishes contain unique stuffings, and the sauces too are unusual and excellent.

I decided to combat the wintry bite in the air with a Squash Apple Bisque, a flavorful soup. Although the hearty Cheese and Egg Strada is the proverbial meal in itself, I was persuaded to try the New England Pudding for dessert. As one born and raised in Connecticut, I've had many versions of this treat, and I must say that Pace One's adaptation, served steaming hot with a scoop of rich vanilla ice cream, is superlative.

Next time I visit Pace One, it will be for dinner, though I know I'll have trouble choosing between Lobster, Shrimp and Crabmeat Casserole (baked in a lobster shell) and Stuffed Filet Mignon (filled with apple, black bread and sausage moistened with Madeira wine). For game lovers, there is Pheasant, roasted and served with a sauce of oranges, black pepper and brandy.

Desserts include Chocolate Fondue, Lemon Cheesecake, Carrot Cake and Double Chocolate Mint Pie served with whipped cream and raspberry sauce.

Much is made of New American Cuisine, forged in restaurants where the personality of the owner or chef takes precedence over classic cookery. Pace One is such a restaurant, designed and run as a reflection of its creative owner.—C.W.

Pace One Restaurant is located in Thornton, two miles from U.S. 1. Lunch is served from 11:30 a.m. until 2:00 p.m., Tuesday through Friday. Dinner is served from 5:30 p.m. until 10:00 p.m., Tuesday through Saturday, and from 5:00 p.m. until 9:00 p.m. on Sunday. Sunday brunch is served from 10:30 a.m. until 2:30 p.m. For reservations (suggested) call (215) 459-9784.

PACE ONE RESTAURANT'S SQUASH APPLE BISQUE

2 apples, peeled and cored
1 small butternut squash, peeled and seeded
6 cups chicken stock
1 small onion, diced
½ teaspoon dried rosemary
1 stick margarine
½ cup flour
milk to taste (optional)

Grate apples and squash on a medium grater. Place chicken stock in a large pot and add the apples, squash, onions and rosemary. Bring to a boil, then lower heat and simmer 30 minutes. Meanwhile, in a small saucepan, melt margarine. Allow to cool without solidifying. Whisk in flour and return

23

saucepan to low heat. Cook, stirring constantly, for about 7 minutes, until mixture changes to a lighter color. Pour into the contents of the large pot in a fine stream, stirring with a whisk until smoothly blended. Simmer soup for 15 minutes. Milk may be added to adjust consistency. Serves 6 to 8.

PACE ONE RESTAURANT'S NEW ENGLAND PUDDING

3 pounds canned chunk pineapple, thoroughly drained

4 apples, cored and cut into chunks

1½ cup walnut meats, coarsely chopped

1 cup brown sugar

4 eggs

2 cups granulated sugar

2 cups flour

¾ pound sweet butter, melted

vanilla ice cream

Preheat oven to 325 degrees. Mix pineapple and apples and place in a 12x7x2-inch pan. Mix walnuts and brown sugar and spread on top of fruits. Whip eggs, add granulated sugar and blend. Add flour and butter to the egg mixture and mix well. Spread batter over fruit, concentrating it on the center of the pan. Bake until golden brown, about 25 minutes. Spoon into bowls and serve with vanilla ice cream. Serves 12.

TOWNE HALL
West Chester

TOWNE HALL

West Chester got a new town hall in 1912, and it got a new restaurant called Towne Hall in 1983. Irate citizens and errant drivers with traffic tickets to pay no longer pass through the massive doors of the former municipal building that has now become a polished restaurant.

What was once the tax collector's office is now the cocktail lounge, bright with shining brass and gleaming wood. What had been the dreary police station is now a beautiful dining room with flowered wallpaper, white nappery and subdued lights.

Upstairs, the former borough manager's office has become a private dining room. The former city council chambers, once the scene of many an emotion-packed council meeting, has become a haven for candlelight dinners. And what was once the mayor's office is the Victorian Lounge, a lively luncheon spot.

Owners Evan and Linda Sharpless scoured the Pennsylvania countryside for the right antiques. They selected Victorian-style chairs and tables, period wallpapers and discreet carpets to be suitable mates for authentic nineteenth-century decorative pieces. They supervised the painstaking stripping of the rare chestnut woodwork. Beneath the fourteen-foot ceilings, the fruits of their labors are abundantly evident, for Towne Hall really is a treasure.

West Chester is the county seat, making Towne Hall popular with judges, lawyers and administrators at lunch. The midday menu features pasta, sandwiches and salads as well as more substantial entrées.

Towne Hall expands on its luncheon offerings at dinner time. The menu, rich with specialties from Switzerland and northern Italy, includes Chicken Tortellini Soup, vegetable-studded Pasta Primavera and rich Pasta Carbonaro. There are Sweet Breads Sautéed in Olive Oil, Garlic and Capers. Veal is prepared four tempting ways, and Towne Hall is one of the few restaurants that serves Baby Rack of Lamb with Mustard Sauce for one.

In spite of the pastas and rich sauces that leap off the menu—and onto the thighs—Towne Hall offers a good selection for weight-watchers. Among the appetizers, Smoked Salmon, Shrimp or Crabmeat Cocktail, Clams or Oysters and Pickled Herring are all low in calories. The Broiled Seafood Combination, consisting of flounder, stuffed shrimp, clams casino, scallops, oyster and lobster is far less of a dieter's downfall than the more common fried version.—c.w.

Towne Hall is located at 15 South High Street in West Chester. Lunch is served from 11:30 a.m. until 2:00 p.m., Monday through Friday. Dinner is served from 5:30 p.m. until 10:00 p.m., Monday through Saturday. For reservations (suggested) call (215) 692-6200.

TOWNE HALL'S OYSTERS ROCKEFELLER

2 garlic cloves, minced
½ pound sweet butter
4 anchovies
1 cup unbleached flour
2 cups milk
1 cup chicken stock
2 tablespoons dry vermouth
2 tablespoons brandy
1 teaspoon salt

½ teaspoon white pepper
½ teaspoon sugar
1 teaspoon lemon juice
2 cups fresh spinach,
    washed, stemmed and
    coarsely chopped
24 fresh oysters (reserve
    24 half-shells)

In a medium saucepan, sauté garlic in butter until garlic is brown. Add anchovies and stir until dissolved. Whisk in flour, stirring until mixture becomes a dark brown roux. Meanwhile, in another saucepan, bring milk to boiling. Remove roux from heat and stir in boiling milk. Return to heat and blend in chicken stock, vermouth, brandy, salt, pepper, sugar and lemon juice, stirring until cream sauce reaches a medium-thick consistency. Preheat oven to 350 degrees. In a saucepan with a tight-fitting lid, briefly steam spinach in the water clinging to the leaves from washing. Drain spinach thoroughly. Blend cream sauce and spinach. Coat oysters with the spinach cream sauce. Place one oyster in each reserved oyster shell half. Place on a baking sheet and bake for 5 to 10 minutes. Serves 6.

TOWNE HALL'S SHRIMP SAVANNAH

½ pound sweet butter
1 cup flour
2 cups milk
1 teaspoon chopped red
  pepper
2 tablespoons dry sherry
1½ teaspoons lemon juice
½ cup grated Parmesan
  cheese

1 teaspoon salt (or to taste)
½ teaspoon sugar
1 cup Hollandaise sauce
  (recipe below)
24 medium shrimp, peeled
  and boiled until pink
grated Parmesan cheese and
  fresh chopped parsley

In a medium saucepan, melt butter. Whisk in flour, stirring until the roux turns light tan. Meanwhile, bring milk to a boil. Add milk, peppers, sherry, lemon juice, Parmesan, salt, sugar and Hollandaise sauce to roux, whisking until smooth and thoroughly blended. Place 6 cooked shrimp in each of 4 individual casseroles. Spoon sauce over shrimp. Sprinkle with grated Parmesan cheese and garnish with parsley. Serves 4.

Hollandaise Sauce:

3 egg yolks
1 to 2 teaspoons cold water
1½ sticks sweet butter,
  melted

dash of cayenne
pinch of salt
1 tablespoon lemon juice or
  tarragon vinegar

In the top of a double boiler over hot (not boiling) water, whisk egg yolks and water until slightly thickened. Gradually add melted butter. When the mixture has thickened into a cream consistency, remove from heat and whisk in cayenne, salt and lemon juice or vinegar. Keep Hollandaise sauce warm over the pilot light of a gas range or in a pan of lukewarm water while preparing the remainder of the recipe.

DULING-KURTZ HOUSE
Exton

DULING-KURTZ HOUSE

The handsome Duling-Kurtz House is an example of the stylistic heights to which a restaurant in which substantial time, money and taste have been invested can rise. The developers, Raymond H. Carr and David J. Knauer, named the restaurant and adjacent bed-and-breakfast inn after their mothers, Edith Duling Carr and Lena Kurtz Knauer.

The restaurant, located on part of a tract of land William Penn granted to Richard Thomas in 1683, is thoughtfully designed, with a myriad of interesting and clever details. The coat checkroom is fronted by old leaded-glass cabinet doors. The exterior of a huge beehive oven, original to the house, is now the focal point of the lounge, a later addition. The bar is made of Chester County walnut, and the barstools were custom-made to match.

Each dining room has a particular atmosphere and is furnished with quality reproductions of antique furniture—Chippendale in this one, Queen Anne in that, Windsor chairs here, ladderbacks there—with carefully chosen antiques as decorative accents. The Tavern Room, all ceiling beams and rustic touches, is a warm haven on a cold winter's night. Aunt Lena's Parlor has pale yellow walls and an elegant oriental rug, and some of Mrs. Knauer's bonnets hang on the walls like artwork. The Hunt Room resembles a men's club, its dark green and white walls decorated with hunting prints.

The Porch, light and bright, has a pleasant garden view, but my favorite nook is the Duling-Kurtz Room, a small curtained-off niche with one very private table for no more than four diners. Usually, it's a romantic twosome that books this *salon privé* overlooking Whitelands Marsh Creek.

The table settings and the service are the same high quality as the décor. I identified the flatware as an early Federalist pattern, and a crystal knife rest at each place is a rare European touch in so American a setting. A glass chimney encircles a silver candlestick on the table, making a lovely couple with the spray of flowers. Fresh popovers, hollow and steaming, are served from a basket with all-too-tempting frequency during cocktails.

I visited twice, and each time the menu had changed almost entirely. The first time, I sampled a satisfying Mushroom Soup, followed by Pork Chops garnished with a fine Stuffed Tomato. The second time, I tried Sautéed Chicken Livers with Mushrooms and Onions, Rack of Lamb, and a salad of spinach, avocado and pine nuts.

When I last dined at the Duling-Kurtz House, I was seated on the Porch, with the pleasant buzz of conversation humming around me and the attractive grounds fading into the twilight.—c.w.

The Duling-Kurtz House is located on South Whitford Road in Exton. Lunch is served from 11:30 a.m. until 2:00 p.m., Monday through Saturday. Dinner is served from 5:30 p.m. until 10:00 p.m., Monday through Thursday, and from 5:30 p.m. until 11:00 p.m. on Friday and Saturday. Sunday brunch is served from 10:30 a.m. until 2:30 p.m. For reservations (recommended) call (215) 524-1830.

DULING-KURTZ HOUSE'S WILD MUSHROOMS, FINES HERBES

2 cups heavy cream
½ pound sweet butter, clarified
3 teaspoons minced garlic
4 pieces of French bread, cut on a diagonal into sections about 5 inches long
4 tablespoons sweet butter
4 ounces oyster mushrooms,* chopped
4 ounces chanterelles,* chopped

4 ounces shiitake mushrooms,* chopped
4 teaspoons shallots
2 tablespoons mixed *fines herbes* (tarragon, chives, chervil and basil)
salt and pepper to taste
1 teaspoon chopped parsley
4 fresh basil leaves

31

In a saucepan over low heat, heat cream until reduced to 1 cup; set aside. In a heavy skillet, heat clarified butter. Add garlic. Sauté for a few minutes until garlic begins to expand. Add bread to skillet and sauté on both sides until well coated with butter and turning light brown. Remove and place on four small plates. In a separate skillet, melt remaining butter. Add mushrooms and sauté, stirring frequently, for 2 minutes. Add shallots and herbs and continue to sauté, stirring frequently, for 1 minute. Add cream. Bring to a boil and continue cooking until liquid is reduced by half. Add salt and pepper to taste. Spoon over garlic bread and garnish each portion with chopped parsley and a fresh basil leaf. Serves 4.

*If unavailable, any fresh mushrooms may be used.

DULING-KURTZ HOUSE'S MANGO SOUP

4 ripe mangoes, peeled and seeded

3 tablespoons Grand Marnier

1 pint heavy cream

6 tablespoons essence (see note)

2 tablespoons honey or sugar (or to taste)

Place the mango pulp in a food processor fitted with a steel blade. Add liquids and process until smooth. Taste for sweetness. Add honey or sugar to taste if necessary. Serves 4.

NOTE: To make essence, boil ¼ cup plus 2 tablespoons water with 2 cloves, 1 cinnamon stick, 1 bay leaf and 3 tablespoons sugar until reduced to ⅓ cup, then strain.

VICKERS TAVERN
Lionville

VICKERS TAVERN

In 1823, a forty-three-year-old potter named John Vickers purchased for eight hundred dollars the farmhouse he had been renting, along with five acres. There he made earthenware, marked Vickers Pottery, which was distributed throughout the Schuylkill Valley and today is prized by collectors of early American ceramics. Vickers also became famous as an abolitionist and a key agent on the Underground Railroad, which smuggled runaway slaves to freedom in the North. He hid escapees in a cooled-down pottery kiln, in a woodpile or in a crawl space under what is now the bar of Vickers Tavern. "Thy Friend Pot" was the way Vickers signed his letters of introduction to the next agent up the line.

If you drive up in the morning, you will find an unprepossessing old farmhouse. Chickens roam the lawn, as they probably did when the Vickers family was in residence, and the atmosphere is decidedly rural. However, at night, when the candles are lit and the tables are set with crisp linens and sparkling glassware, this is not only a historic restaurant but a sophisticated one as well. The menu is Continental— and so is the host, a charming extrovert named Arturo Burigatto, who has managed the old Vickers property since 1972 and owned it since 1977.

My friends and I were fortunate that Arturo had some time to sit down and chat while we feasted on one of everything from the hors d'oeuvres cart, various entrées and a sampling of several fine pastries. My Escalope de Veau aux Morilles, a thick oval of veal sautéed with a sublime cream sauce rich in morels, was one of the finest veal entrées I've ever tasted.

Even though his background is far removed from the Quaker abolitionists who once owned the property, and his tastes far more lavish than their spare lifestyle, Arturo is as respectful of history and tradition as anyone who grew up in Venice must be. He therefore has a potter's wheel at the entrance to the restaurant, and he hires a craftsperson to run it, making distinctive ashtrays, candleholders and other small items in the tradition of "Thy Friend Pot."—c.w.

34

Vickers Tavern is located at Welsh Pool Road and Gordon Drive in Lionville. Lunch is served from 11:30 a.m. until 2:00 p.m., Monday through Friday. Dinner is served from 5:30 p.m. until 11:00 p.m., Monday through Saturday. For reservations (suggested) call (215) 363-6336.

VICKERS TAVERN'S ESCALOPE DE VEAU AUX MORILLES

25 morels
Madeira wine
12 2-ounce medallions of
   veal, cut from the fillet
salt and pepper to taste
3 ounces clarified butter
flour
2 tablespoons finely minced
   shallots

½ ounce balsamic vinegar
3 ounces Madeira wine
8 ounces demi-glace (reduc-
   tion of veal stock)
3 ounces heavy cream
3 tablespoons sweet butter

Soak morels in Madeira wine to cover for 30 minutes. Season veal with salt and pepper and flatten slightly with the side of a cleaver or a meat pounder. Heat a large skillet and add the clarified butter. Drench medallions in flour on one side and place them in the skillet, floured side first. Sauté two minutes on each side, until lightly browned. Remove to heated dish and set aside. Add shallots to skillet and cook for 1 minute, stirring occasionally to prevent burning. Deglaze skillet with balsamic vinegar and Madeira wine. Reduce liquid over high heat, stirring, until the consistency of cream. Lower heat and stir in demi-glace and heavy cream. Stir in butter and mix well. Add veal, morels and the Madeira wine in which they were soaked; heat through. Place veal on serving platter and pour sauce over. Serves 4.

VICKERS TAVERN'S ALMOND TORTE

3 ounces marzipan
5 egg yolks

3 ounces flour
3 ounces almond, ground

6 ounces sweet butter,
softened
5 ounces sugar
pinch of salt
dash of vanilla extract
pinch of grated lemon rind
pinch of cinnamon
4 egg whites
3 ounces superfine sugar

Rum Syrup (recipe below)
1 small jar of apricot preserves, boiled and
strained
Almond Butter Cream
(recipe below)
3 ounces toasted almond
slivers

Preheat oven to 375 degrees. Beat together marzipan and egg yolks until well mixed. Add butter, sugar, salt, vanilla, lemon rind and cinnamon. Beat egg whites until soft peaks form. Mix in sugar and continue beating until stiff. Carefully fold into the first mixture and mix in flour and ground almonds. Pour into a buttered and floured 9-inch cake pan. Bake for 50 minutes. Cool and remove from cake pan. Cut into 3 even slices and soak lightly with Rum Syrup. Apply apricot preserves lightly on one layer. Top with Almond Butter Cream. Add a second layer and repeat the process. Top with third layer and garnish with toasted almonds. Yields one 9-inch torte.

Rum Syrup:
½ cup water
1 cup sugar

½ cup rum

Heat water with sugar until just boiling. Stir in rum. Cool.

Almond Butter Cream:
3 eggs, unbeaten
9 egg whites, unbeaten
¾ cup water
2 cups sugar

1½ pounds sweet butter,
softened
½ teaspoon almond extract

Place unbeaten eggs and egg whites into a large bowl. Boil water and sugar together to soft ball stage. Pour boiling syrup straight into eggs and egg whites while beating. Continue beating until the mixture is cool. Beat in butter, bit by bit, and add almond extract.

THE JEFFERSON HOUSE RESTAURANT
Norristown

THE JEFFERSON HOUSE RESTAURANT

Can fate strike twice? It did for Angelo Romano. When Romano, the owner of The Jefferson House Restaurant, was seventeen years old, he was apprenticed to Master Chef Henry Sidoli at Philadelphia's Warwick Hotel. One day Romano's idol, baseball hero Joe DiMaggio, came into the Warwick and ordered a hamburger. Chef Sidoli decided that the time had come to give Romano the test of his career. The chef told his apprentice to prepare a seven-course meal for DiMaggio.

Needless to say, the young culinary wizard gave his all to the project. DiMaggio, impressed with the feast, asked to meet the chef. The ballplayer predicted that one day the young man's talent would reward him with the ownership of his own restaurant. Romano replied, "Mr. DiMaggio, if that comes true, then I will owe you another dinner."

Thirty-five years later, DiMaggio came to dinner at The Jefferson House, unaware that Romano was the owner. In honor of this astonishing coincidence, Romano couldn't resist preparing the most elaborate meal that he could devise. Once again, DiMaggio was overwhelmed. Afterward, Romano would not allow the ballplayer to pay for the meal because, he said, it was part of a thirty-five-year-old promise. As Romano started to explain, DiMaggio remembered the occasion, stopped him, and finished telling the story exactly as it had occurred.

I heard this anecdote as I sat in the garden room of the magnificent 1848 Georgian mansion, once the home of the Cunard family of the famous cruise line. When I sampled Romano's wares, I was as impressed as DiMaggio.

Because I've never been known to bypass Escargot, I opted for their tasty creation in puff pastry. I also took just a sample of Black Bean Soup and found it rich and hearty beyond all my expectations. The soup was followed by a Tossed Salad with their House Dressing, a creamy delicacy laced with herbs.

The choice of an entrée was difficult, but I had never tried Chicken Florentine, so I ordered this scrumptious dish of chicken filled with ricotta cheese on a bed of sautéed spinach.

For those watching their spreading waistlines, a lighter selection would be the Rack of Lamb with Herb Mustard. The restaurant will also accommodate any medical or religious diet, within reason.

I enjoyed the house Chablis and noted that the restaurant's wine list is well chosen, but quite inexpensive for an establishment of this stature.

The murderous decision was dessert. When I tasted their White Chocolate Mousse with Strawberry Sauce, I wanted that recipe. But when the Black Velvet Cake crossed my palate, the old taste buds declared that creation the winner instead. However, I must say that this entire restaurant is a winner, from its gentle ambience to its creative cuisine.

The Jefferson House Restaurant is located at 2519 DeKalb Pike in Norristown. Lunch is served from 11:30 a.m. until 2:30 p.m., Monday through Friday. Dinner is served from 4:30 p.m. until 10:00 p.m., Monday through Saturday. Sunday dinner is served from 1:00 p.m. until 8:00 p.m. For reservations (suggested) call (215) 275-3407.

THE JEFFERSON HOUSE RESTAURANT'S
BLACK VELVET CAKE

Sponge cake:

1¾ cup all-purpose flour	1 stick butter, melted
1 cup cornstarch	½ teaspoon vanilla
12 eggs	½ teaspoon lemon extract
3 cups sugar	

Sift flour and cornstarch together twice; set aside. Whip eggs and sugar together over a double boiler until mixture is warm. Transfer mixture to bowl of an electric mixer and mix on medium speed until volume increases. Reduce mixer speed to low and slowly add flour-cornstarch mixture. Combine butter with vanilla and lemon extract and add to batter, mixing until just incorporated. Grease two 9x12-inch sheet pans, pour batter evenly into pans and bake at 350 degrees for approximately 20 minutes or until cake springs back to the touch.

Mousse Filling:

8 ounces semisweet chocolate, chopped fine	½ cup sugar
¼ cup hot coffee	1 package unflavored gelatin
5 eggs, separated	2 tablespoons vanilla

In the top of double boiler, place chocolate and coffee. Heat until chocolate melts, then let cool. Whip egg yolks until pale yellow and combine with chocolate mixture. In a separate bowl whip egg whites with sugar until soft peaks form. Gently fold into chocolate. Whip in gelatin and vanilla until combined. Refrigerate until mousse sets up.

Icing:

2 cups heavy whipping cream	32 ounces semisweet chocolate, chopped fine

Bring cream to a boil and add chocolate. Remove from heat and stir until mixed. Refrigerate until mixture thickens slightly. This icing does not become very thick.

Assembly:

Take sponge cake and cut one 4x9-inch strip to form the side of the cake. Also cut one 9-inch circle and one 7-inch circle. In a 9- or 9½-inch springform pan, lay the 9-inch circle on the bottom; place the 4-inch strip around the side of the pan (it will be resting on top of the bottom layer), cutting away any excess cake. Fill the center with chocolate mousse. Place the 7-inch circle on top of the mousse (this layer will fit down within the side strip). Spread a layer of icing on top and return cake to refrigerator for two hours to set. After it sets, slide a knife around the edge to loosen the cake, and turn it upside down. Spread icing around sides and over top (which was bottom layer before inversion). Serve chilled. Yields 1 large cake.

NOTE: This cake may be served with 1 cup of whipped cream laced with 1 tablespoon Grand Marnier. This recipe can successfully be divided in half by using one 9x12-inch pan and assembling the cake in an 8-inch springform pan.

WILLIAM PENN INN
Gwnedd

WILLIAM PENN INN Getting the job you dreamed of as a child isn't always a reality, as some temporary employees of William Penn Inn learned a few years ago. When the inn, which has been in operation since 1714, opened their Colonial Seafood Dining Room, proprietor Peter Friedrich wanted to alert the public to this event with an attention-getting promotion. A man-sized lobster suit, complete with claws, was constructed for a young man to wear as he waved to passersby in front of the elegant old restaurant. Unfortunately, half an hour after "Lobster-Man" went public with the restaurant's statement, Friedrich found the costume in the men's room, sans occupant. As he was mulling over the problem, another young man appeared looking for work. Yes, you guessed it—ten minutes later the new Lobster-Man was on his beat, doing something I'm sure he would never have envisioned as a career.

The garden-style room where we dined overlooked the same street that brought William Penn and his daughter, Letitia, to this inn for an overnight stay sometime around 1700. The inn was at that time the private residence of Thomas Evans, a Welsh Quaker whom Penn visited while traveling from Philadelphia to the Penn home on the Delaware River.

My companion, Chrissy White, and I began with a Robert Mondavi White Chardonnay, which lent the right dry taste to complement their delectable Crab Imperial Stuffed Mushrooms resting in Lobster Sauce. We also sampled a Salmon Mousse, which was unlike any we had ever tasted, and their absolutely delicious Fettuccine Commonwealth, a combination of shrimp, bay scallops, lobster and crab, topped with a white sauce and nested in fettucini.

Of course I had to have a taste of their delicious Snapper Soup, which was, as promised, different from any other in Pennsylvania. A green salad followed, with a sassy Tarragon Dressing that I knew would be a hit recipe.

My entrée was a fresh and luscious Crabmeat Commonwealth. Chrissy chose Red Snapper broiled in wine and herbs, which turned out to be as delicious as it was virtuous for those of us who can't afford to squander calories. Both were served with a luscious loaf of Zucchini Bread.

We couldn't squeeze in dessert, but I won't pass up their Chocolate Mousse and Strawberry Cheesecake the next time I visit this gracious restaurant.

William Penn Inn is located on Rt. 202 and Sumneytown Pike in Gwnedd. Lunch is served from 11:30 a.m. until 3:00 p.m., Monday through Saturday. Dinner is served from 5:00 p.m. until 10:00 p.m., Monday through Thursday; from 5:00 p.m. until 11:00 p.m., Friday and Saturday; and from 3:00 p.m. until 8:00 p.m. on Sunday. Sunday brunch is served from 11:00 a.m. until 3:00 p.m. For reservations (preferred) call (215) 699-9272.

WILLIAM PENN INN'S FETTUCCINE COMMONWEALTH

4 teaspoons clarified butter
½ clove garlic, diced
1 teaspoon chopped shallot
12 medium shrimp, cleaned
½ pound bay scallops
6 ounces Snow Crab leg meat

¼ cup white wine
1 cup heavy cream
½ cup grated Parmesan cheese
1 egg yolk
salt and pepper to taste
½ pound cooked fettucini

Place butter in a skillet over medium heat and sauté garlic and shallots until translucent. Add shrimp, scallops and meat from crab legs and sauté 2 or 3 minutes. Remove mixture from skillet and reserve in a warm place. Drain skillet and deglaze with wine; add cream and cheese. Reduce heat and stir frequently to keep from sticking. When sauce is slightly thickened, remove from heat and stir in egg yolk. Season with salt and pepper to taste. Return to range and heat through. Pour seafood over fettucini and top with sauce. Serves 4.

WILLIAM PENN INN'S ZUCCHINI BREAD

2 eggs
1 cup sugar

½ teaspoon baking powder
1 cup grated zucchini

43

½ cup vegetable oil
1½ cups plus 2 tablespoons flour
¾ teaspoon baking soda
¾ teaspoon salt

½ teaspoon ground cinnamon
½ cup raisins
½ cup chopped walnuts
½ teaspoon vanilla

With electric mixer on medium speed, beat eggs and gradually beat in sugar. Add oil, beating until well combined. Sift together dry ingredients and add to egg mixture alternately with zucchini. Stir in raisins, chopped walnuts and vanilla, mixing to incorporate. Grease and flour a 1-pound loaf pan; pour mixture into pan. Bake in a preheated 350-degree oven for 55 minutes. Yields 1 loaf.

NOTE: This bread freezes well.

WILLIAM PENN INN'S TARRAGON DRESSING

1 scant teaspoon dried minced tarragon
1 cup water
½ teaspoon salt
1¾ tablespoon sugar
2 teaspoons garlic powder

pinch of cayenne pepper
4½ teaspoons tarragon vinegar
1 cup mayonnaise
2 tablespoons milk

Place dried tarragon and water in a small saucepan. Bring to a boil and let boil about 1 minute. Drain tarragon through a strainer and set aside. In a small container combine salt, sugar, garlic powder, cayenne and tarragon vinegar and let stand for 10 minutes. Add mayonnaise, blending thoroughly. Add milk and drained tarragon and stir until well mixed. Refrigerate. Yields about 1 cup.

GENERAL WAYNE INN
Merion

GENERAL WAYNE INN

Great howling is heard every time the post office raises rates, but flip backward for a look at the colonial postal system and your howling becomes a murmur. In our country's early years, it was the mail recipient who paid for postage. Each letter was weighed for amount and distance and had to be paid for in cash at rates that are high by today's standards. Can you imagine paying for all the junk mail we receive today?

At the General Wayne Inn, I sat in a dining room called the Franklin Post Office. This room operated as a post office from 1704 until 1897. Today, its name commemorates Benjamin Franklin, who, as Postmaster General for England's American colonies, came here in 1763 and supervised the handling of the mail.

Originally known as the Wayside Inn, this inn functioned not only as a post office but also as a stagecoach stop, general store, tavern, hotel, restaurant and seller of lottery tickets. Its guest book reads like the *Who's Who* of colonial America. Represented are George Washington, Benjamin Franklin, General William Howe, General Anthony Wayne and Captain Allan McLane.

Not far from the inn, on a hill to the west, one of the lesser-known battles of the Revolutionary War did *not* take place on September 16, 1777. On that day, Nature entered the combat in the form of a blinding rainstorm. On neither side could the soldiers spark the wet gunpowder with their flints. The interrupted skirmish was dubbed "The Battle of the Clouds," and records show that the inn had standing room only for the rest of the day.

The following year, Captain Allan McLane used the elements to his advantage to fool the British. In a knee-deep snowfall, McLane, with the aid of the Iroquois Indians, camouflaged his troops with white sheets and recaptured the inn from the Redcoats.

But it was General Wayne for whom the inn was renamed in 1795, following a reception held there in his honor. Hosted by three troops of Philadelphia Light Horse, the reception celebrated the general's victory over hostile Indian tribes at the Battle of Fallen Timber.

Many years after the Revolution, the General Wayne Inn continued to receive famous visitors. It was here that Edgar Allan Poe, seated in a darkened corner of the post office, imbibed as he wrote passages of "The Raven." You probably wouldn't think of Poe as one to indulge in graffiti, but in 1843 he chiseled his initials on—and thereby immortalized—one of the window panes.

Seated near Poe's window, I indulged in food that was typical of colonial fare. The day was a nip chilly, which made their Philadelphia Pepper Pot Soup all the more inviting. This appetizing restorer was quickly followed by a yummy Baked Crabmeat au Gratin. A side dish of old-fashioned Stewed Tomatoes and Okra was reminiscent of some Cajun recipes I've tried, without being quite so spicy.

Judging from the paintings of that era, I don't think the colonists watched their waistlines, but the General Wayne Inn does help those who feel the need today. A special Diet Corner listed on their menu includes a Tuna or Turkey Salad as well as Chopped Sirloin.

After my own filling repast, I couldn't squeeze in dessert, but next time I'll remember not to eat so much, so that I can enjoy their Apricot Mousse!

The General Wayne Inn is located at 625 Montgomery Avenue in Merion. Lunch is served from 11:30 a.m. until 2:00 p.m., Tuesday through Saturday. Dinner is served from 5:00 p.m. until midnight, Tuesday through Saturday; On Sunday, brunch is served from 11:30 a.m. until 2:30 p.m.; dinner is served from 4:00 p.m. until 9:00 p.m. For reservations (preferred) call (215) 664-5125.

THE GENERAL WAYNE INN'S BAKED CRABMEAT AU GRATIN

1 pound lump crabmeat	dash of Tabasco sauce
½ cup all-purpose flour	dash of Worcestershire sauce

¼ cup melted butter
2 cups half and half
3 ounces sharp white
   cheese, grated

dash of salt
¾ cup bread crumbs

Preheat oven to 350 degrees. Spread crabmeat on a tray and place in oven until shells turn white (about 5 minutes). Pick shells from meat and set crabmeat aside. In a saucepan over low heat blend flour and butter to make a roux; reduce heat to medium and add half and half, stirring until roux is smooth. Add cheese, Tabasco Sauce, Worcestershire Sauce and salt; stir until cheese has melted. Fold crabmeat into sauce. Place mixture in a greased 2-quart casserole and sprinkle with bread crumbs. Bake in a 400-degree oven until bread crumbs are brown (14 to 20 minutes). Serves 4 to 6.

THE GENERAL WAYNE INN'S STEWED TOMATOES WITH OKRA

1 14½-ounce can whole
   tomatoes in juice
1½ tablespoons cornstarch
1 7½-ounce can diced okra

¼ cup sugar
dash of salt
6 slices white bread, cubed

Place tomatoes with their juice in a saucepan. Remove ¼ cup of juice and blend with cornstarch in a small saucepan; set aside. Drain okra (discard juice) and wash under cold water; let drain. Bring tomatoes with their remaining juice to a boil and add cornstarch mixture, stirring to incorporate. Reduce heat to medium-low and blend in sugar. Add salt, okra and bread cubes. Pour into a greased 1½- to 2-quart baking dish and bake at 400 degrees for 20 minutes. Serves 4.

THE OLD ORIGINAL BOOKBINDER'S
RESTAURANT
Philadelphia

BOOKBINDER'S RESTAURANT

Because a surname often refers to the family's original occupation, I was intrigued when I heard of Bookbinder's Restaurant in Philadelphia. I thought that the restaurant's site had once been part of a publishing department that bound books.

Actually, bookbinding equipment was about the only thing I didn't find in this multi-faceted restaurant. Located just around the corner from William Penn's home, the restaurant was opened by Samuel Bookbinder in 1865. Beside the front door stands Sarah Bookbinder's bell, once used as a signal to nearby merchants and dockworkers that her famous seafood was ready. Fortunately, fresh seafood remained on the menu even after the restaurant's management passed into the hands of the Bookbinders' son, Manny. While serving time for bootlegging, this well-organized character arranged to be released from jail every night in order to check on the restaurant's cash flow.

I myself was greeted, not by the ringing bell, but by a saltwater tank full of live lobsters. True to the restaurant's tradition, the cuisine remains fresh and simple. Proprietor John Taxin's philosophy is to "buy the best and do as little to it as possible."

Seated in the President's Dining Room, I observed that every inch of wall space was occupied by portraits of American presidents who have dined here. Co-proprietor Albert Taxin told me that this dining room was Frank Sinatra's favorite. This frequent guest wanted his picture hung with the presidents rather than with the celebrities. Jokingly, Taxin told Sinatra that he was missing two credentials: the presidency and a beard. A month later Taxin received the singer's portrait, complete with beard. Today you'll see Sinatra's whiskered likeness hanging with the presidents—but above the kitchen door.

Passing into an adjoining room, I found the walls lined with an extensive collection of antique trains, toy banks and guns. The weapons are displayed as a reminder that guns were made in this same room during the Civil War.

Back at my table, I began with Snapper Soup, my first taste of this Pennsylvania favorite made from snapping turtles. It is a wonderfully rich and hearty soup to have on a cold day. I found the Shrimp du Jour, sautéed in garlic butter and topped with cheese, to be a winning creation, but my very favorite selection (which turned out to be the ideal diet choice) was Jumbo Shrimp steamed in red pepper flakes. Ummm! Spicy, hot and delicious.

You wouldn't believe me if I described it, so you'll have to go and see their Coconut Cake, which stands eight inches high. I sampled this delectable fantasy, along with their wonderful Apple Walnut Pie.

I was satisfied with hot tea, but Bookbinder's does offer their special alcoholic brews, as well as a variety of quality wines.

I left with the impression that Bookbinder's is much more than a restaurant. It's a museum of American toys, guns and Lincoln memorabilia, in the midst of which is served food so fresh that "you taste the fish, not the sauce."

The Old Original Bookbinder's Restaurant is located at 125 Walnut Street in Philadelphia. Lunch is served from 11:45 a.m. until 2:45 p.m., Monday through Friday. Dinner is served from 2:45 p.m. until 10:00 p.m., Monday through Friday; from noon until 10:00 p.m. on Saturday; and from 1:00 p.m. until 9:00 p.m. on Sunday. For reservations (suggested) call (215) 925-7027.

THE OLD ORIGINAL BOOKBINDER'S RESTAURANT'S JUMBO SHRIMP

2 cups water (approximately)

4 to 6 teaspoons white vinegar

3 to 4 teaspoons red pepper flakes

20 jumbo shrimp

Place 2 inches of water in a steamer and add vinegar and red pepper flakes. If more water is needed for steamer, increase vinegar and red pepper flakes; if less is needed, decrease. Put

51

unshelled shrimp in steamer colander, cover and steam for 15 to 25 minutes, depending on size of shrimp. After 15 minutes, peel one to test for doneness. When shrimp is done it will be pink and tender. May serve with cocktail sauce if desired. Serves 4.

THE OLD ORIGINAL BOOKBINDER'S RESTAURANT'S APPLE WALNUT PIE

Crust:

1¾ cups flour   1 teaspoon cinnamon
¼ cup sugar   1 stick butter

Combine dry ingredients, and cut in the butter with two knives or a pastry blender until well mixed. Roll out crust and place in a 10-inch springform pan.

Filling:

2 cups sour cream   ½ cup flour
2 eggs, lightly beaten   2 teaspoons vanilla
1 cup sugar   6 large apples, peeled
pinch of salt   and sliced

Mix first six ingredients together until thoroughly combined, then stir apples into mixture. Pour mixture into the unbaked crust. Bake at 450 degrees for 10 minutes, reduce heat to 350 degrees, stir filling, and bake 30 to 40 minutes longer.

Topping:

½ cup brown sugar   pinch of salt
½ cup white sugar   1 stick butter, melted
½ cup all-purpose flour   1 cup chopped walnuts
1 teaspoon cinnamon

Blend dry ingredients. Stir in butter and mix until well blended. Add walnuts, stirring until incorporated. Place mixture on top of pie filling. Bake for 15 minutes at 350 degrees. Yields 1 pie.

THE SOCIETY HILL HOTEL,
RESTAURANT AND BAR
Philadelphia

SOCIETY HILL The snow on the street was four inches deep the day I arrived in Philadelphia. When my cab pulled up to The Society Hill Hotel, Restaurant and Bar—well, I wouldn't have believed it if I hadn't seen it, but there were customers arriving on cross-country skis. Others, their skis already parked beside the building, were sitting outside at the sidewalk café, downing hot drinks and scrumptious-looking sandwiches that I was soon to know (and love) as Philadelphia Phenomenon Cheese Steaks.

I felt rather cowardly sitting inside the restaurant watching the fun-loving group celebrating the winter's first snowstorm. I wanted to take in the camaraderie, but at a warm distance, so I lighted on one of the bar-height stools at a table beside the window. I found that the atmosphere inside this neighborhood hangout was equally appealing and festive. Fresh flowers on the wood-and-brass bar, large green plants hanging from the window, and green Tiffany lamps lent color and balance to the woody interior created by dark, terracotta-colored walls and ceiling.

Scribbling notes all the while, I sampled Wang Wings and Arlene's Artichokes along with a glass of fruity Beaujolais. When the manager asked me which recipe I wanted, I agonized over the choice. In the end, I got both.

In the South, customers have often been friendly toward my research, but I had thought Philadelphians would be more reserved. Not so. Friendly customers chatted with me about the restaurant. One group told me about a live jazz band that sometimes plays there. A skier introduced himself as a regular customer and an under-thirty-five Democrat (the media description of the restaurant's clientele) and advised me to try the Cheese Steak. When I sank my teeth into this phenomenon on an Italian roll, I was glad I had taken his advice.

I was also glad for my chic, high-ceilinged suite on the top floor of this four-story establishment. Built as an oyster house in 1832, the building changed occupants a number of times. In 1846, Volney B. Palmer located America's first advertising agency here. During the Civil War it served as a recruiting station, and finally, in the early 1900s, it became a hotel and restaurant. The current owners have done extensive renovation, but have kept intact as much as possible of the original structure and 1830 woodwork.

I felt almost decadent as I luxuriated in my brass bed the following morning, sipping fresh-squeezed orange juice and munching on sweet rolls, a breakfast accompanied by English tea and a bouquet of fresh flowers. I won't soon forget this bed-and-breakfast establishment, a European concept splashed with American friendliness.

The Society Hill Hotel, Restaurant and Bar is located at 301 Chestnut Street in Philadelphia. Meals are served from 11:00 a.m. until 1:00 a.m. daily. Sunday brunch is served from 11:00 a.m. until 2:30 p.m. Reservations are unnecessary, but the telephone number is (215) 925-1919.

THE SOCIETY HILL'S PHILADELPHIA PHENOMENON CHEESE STEAK

1 8-inch, round Italian roll
2 tablespoons vegetable oil
6 ounces thinly sliced steak
2 slices cheese (American, Mozzarella or Provolone)
2 or more tablespoons water
1 tablespoon chopped, sautéed onions (optional)
1 tablespoon chopped, sautéed green peppers (optional)
1 tablespoon chopped, sautéed mushrooms (optional)
1 slice bacon, fried and crumbled (optional)
1 tablespoon chopped artichoke hearts (optional)
1 to 2 tablespoons commercial pizza sauce (optional)

Cut roll in half and hollow out. Heat roll in a 250-degree oven until warm, approximately 4 to 5 minutes. Heat oil on grill or in frying pan. When oil is hot, sizzle steak. (Break steak apart for faster cooking.) When steak has cooked for 10 to 15 seconds, place cheese on top; add water to grill or frying pan to aid cheese in melting. Remove from grill or pan; stuff roll with steak and cheese and any or all of the optional toppings. Serves 1.

THE SOCIETY HILL'S ARLENE'S ARTICHOKES

1 13¾-ounce can of
  artichoke hearts
2 eggs
½ to ¾ cup Italian-seasoned
  bread crumbs

1½ cups oil for deep frying
Garlic Butter (recipe below)

Drain artichoke hearts and cut each in half. Beat eggs. Dip artichoke hearts in beaten egg and coat in bread crumbs. Deep fry for about 30 seconds until golden brown. Remove to serving dish and cover with Garlic Butter. Serves 3.

Garlic Butter:
1 stick butter, softened
dash of salt
1 tablespoon chopped fresh
  parsley

½ teaspoon garlic powder
juice of 1 lemon

Mix softened butter with all ingredients until blended. Refrigerate for use with other vegetables. Yields ¼ cup.

THE SOCIETY HILL'S WANG WINGS

⅔ cup Louisiana hot sauce
2 eggs
1½ tablespoons water
8 chicken wings

flour for dusting
1½ cups vegetable oil
Sour Cream Sauce (recipe
  below)

In a bowl mix hot sauce, eggs and water and stir until combined. Soak chicken wings in mixture for at least 10 minutes. Remove wings and dust with flour. Deep fry at 350 degrees for about 5 minutes. Serve with Sour Cream Sauce. Serves 3 to 4.

Sour Cream Sauce:
¼ cup sour cream
¼ cup buttermilk

⅛ cup Parmesan cheese
pepper to taste

Mix above ingredients well. Refrigerate. Yields ½ cup.

HEAD HOUSE INN
Philadelphia

HEAD HOUSE INN

You may think that ours is the age of the clever wheeler-dealers, but look back and you'll find that our ancestors also did some fast horse-trading. One deal that particularly amuses me was made in Philadelphia in 1771. The city's mayor, Samuel Powell, persuaded area farmers to relocate their market. Coincidentally, the new site he suggested was only one block away from his home in the Society Hill section. Although Powell promised to purchase any perishable food that was not sold at the new location, he rarely had to live up to that end of the bargain, because the new market at Head House Square caught on immediately.

I'll confess that the name Society Hill sounds a bit snobbish, until you learn that it came from an association called The Free Society. This association owned the original William Penn land grant, including the Head House Square–Society Hill area.

The Head House Inn, directly across from the square, was built in 1771 by John McNeal, who hosted members of the Continental Congress, including—oh yes—George Washington. You know, I don't believe that man ever spent a night at home.

It is easy to see the appeal that this inn had for our wandering president. Hanging over the bar are the original oak beams, now over two hundred years old. The random-planked floors are pegged with oak plugs. Owners Scott and Linda Livingston told me that the blue-gray of the walls is an authentic old Philadelphia shade.

The trestle table of my old wooden booth was warmed by a bouquet of fresh flowers, and I was warmed by the inn's Fisherman Chowder, a creamy combination of water chestnuts, clams and shrimp. The chowder got four stars—but when I tasted their Pepper Steak Soup with an oriental flavor, I had to create a five-star category.

Stuffed Mushrooms filled with cream cheese and clams came next. Just one bite prompted me to request the recipe for these tasty morsels.

I have always been a trout lover, and their Trout Almondine

struck me as the ideal choice for those of us who want quality without caloric quantity. Served with the trout was a yummy Butternut Squash with an Orange Raisin Sauce.

When I think of the cute image of the bunny, it's hard for me to order rabbit. However, Head House's Braised Rabbit Hunter Style quickly replaces that image with delicious new ideas.

This restaurant's desserts go beyond sin. The Chocolate Mousse Truffle Cake is so rich that only Diamond Jim Brady could finish a whole piece, although I made excellent inroads. The winning choice, though, was their Cranberry Walnut Bread Pudding, with its unique sweet-tart flavor.

The Head House Inn is located at Second and Pine streets in Philadelphia. Lunch is served from 11:30 a.m. until 4:00 p.m., Monday through Sunday. Dinner is served from 5:00 p.m. until 10:00 p.m., Sunday through Thursday, and from 5:00 p.m. until midnight on Friday and Saturday. Sunday brunch is served from 11:30 a.m. until 4:00 p.m. The tavern is open from 11:30 a.m. until 2:00 a.m. daily. For reservations call (215) 925-6718.

HEAD HOUSE INN'S BRAISED RABBIT HUNTER STYLE

5 to 6 slices bacon
1 2½ pound rabbit
1 small onion, diced
1 green pepper, diced
½ cup diced mushrooms
1 garlic clove, chopped

1 medium tomato, diced
¼ teaspoon thyme
¾ cup red wine
¾ cup brown gravy (commercial or homemade)

In a deep skillet, fry bacon until crisp; remove. Cut up rabbit and braise in bacon grease; remove. Add onion, green pepper, mushrooms, garlic, tomato and thyme, and sauté until tender. Add rabbit, wine and gravy. Crumble bacon and add to mixture. Reduce heat, cover and simmer for 30 minutes. Serves 4.

HEAD HOUSE INN'S PEPPER STEAK SOUP

1 pound top round steak
1½ large green peppers
1 medium onion
2 tablespoons butter
1 tablespoon finely chopped
  ginger
¼ cup white wine

1 quart beef stock (commercial or homemade)
5 ounces soy sauce
salt and pepper to taste
2 tablespoons cornstarch
¼ cup water
1 tablespoon sesame oil

Julienne beef, peppers, and onion. In a large pot sauté beef strips in butter; remove. Quickly sauté peppers, onions and ginger; remove while still crisp. Deglaze pot with white wine, then add beef stock, soy sauce, salt and pepper. Simmer for 30 minutes. Thicken with cornstarch dissolved in water. Add beef, peppers and onions. Return to boil, then simmer for 45 minutes. Add sesame oil just before serving. Yields six 1-cup servings.

HEAD HOUSE INN'S STUFFED MUSHROOMS

1 small can chopped clams,
  drained (save juice)
1 shallot, minced
8 ounces cream cheese,
  softened
dash of Tabasco sauce

2 teaspoons Worcestershire
  sauce
2 teaspoons Dijon mustard
20 to 25 large fresh
  mushrooms
2 tablespoons butter

In a small saucepan simmer 3 to 4 tablespoons of the reserved clam juice with shallots until liquid is reduced by ¾. Cool. Add cream cheese to clam juice mixture and mix well with clams, Tabasco sauce, Worcestershire sauce and mustard. Remove stems from mushrooms and fill each hollow with about 1 tablespoon stuffing. In frying pan, simmer stuffed mushrooms in butter until cooked but still firm. Arrange mushrooms on baking sheet and place under broiler for a minute or so. Serves 4 to 6.

THE CITY TAVERN
Philadelphia

THE CITY TAVERN Today's media, we are told, have influenced our attitudes toward dress and cosmetics to the point of making us a very vain and materialistic society. But a history lesson at The City Tavern, on the site of the original City Tavern where the colonial aristocracy used to meet, taught me the true meaning of vanity. It seems that not only did upper-class colonists adhere meticulously to the fashionable dress of the day, but men and women with pockmarked skin filled their scars with wax, powdering over the face for a natural look.

This story was told to me on a cold, snowy day while I sipped a revitalizing Hot Buttered Rum beside an open Franklin stove. I thought about how those aristocrats must have looked on hot days when the wax began to melt, and I decided that current society isn't such a vain bunch after all.

The original City Tavern played a role not only in colonial society, but in American history as well. In May of 1774, as the breach with Great Britain was widening, some of America's leading citizens held a meeting in the tavern's Long Room that shaped Pennsylvania's response to the Intolerable Acts. Three months later, when John Adams arrived in Philadelphia to attend the First Continental Congress, he was taken first to The City Tavern. Adams described the tavern as "the most genteel in America."

Following the Second Continental Congress, it became the custom of Randolph, Lee, Washington, Harrison, Alsop, Chase, Rodney and Reed to form a "table" and dine at the tavern daily. It is believed that amidst steaming venison and tankards of ale, many of the laws we live by today were first discussed at this "table."

I imbibed the old political tales as I sampled a succulent Rack of Lamb with a piquant Dijon mustard sauce and a wonderful Stuffed Flounder baked in puff pastry. My meal was accented with a glass of Sauvignon Blanc Lambert. The colonists rarely dieted, so I didn't either; but if you stuck to the lamb and vegetables, you could enjoy the ambience of this authentically reconstructed tavern and not gain an ounce.

The City Tavern is located at Second and Walnut streets in Philadelphia. Lunch is served from 11:30 a.m. until 3:30 p.m., daily. Dinner is served from 5:00 p.m. until 9:00 p.m., Sunday through Thursday, and from 5:00 p.m. until 10:00 p.m., Friday and Saturday. For reservations (preferred) call (215) 923-6059.

THE CITY TAVERN'S RACK OF LAMB

1 rack of lamb	1 small garlic clove, diced
6 tablespoons Dijon mustard	1 teaspoon rosemary
2 tablespoons white wine	½ teaspoon white pepper

Trim fat from lamb; French the bones by removing the meat from between the rib bones and scraping bones clean. Preheat oven to 450 degrees. Place lamb fat side down in a roasting pan and bake for 15 minutes. Remove from oven and pour off fat. Lower oven temperature to 400 degrees. In a small bowl, make a paste of mustard, wine, garlic, rosemary and white pepper. Paint mixture over lamb, insert meat thermometer and return to oven; cook at 400 degrees for about 15 minutes. Lamb should be ready when meat thermometer reaches 125 degrees. Meat should be rare. Do not overcook. Serves 2.

THE CITY TAVERN'S FLOUNDER IN CRUST

2 sheets puff pastry (commercial)	½ pound fresh spinach, coarsely chopped
4 tablespoons butter	1 teaspoon coarse black pepper
1 medium onion, coarsely chopped	1 pound deboned fresh flounder
½ pound fresh mushrooms, sliced	1 egg

On a floured board roll out pastry sheets until thin; cut into 4 equal pieces. Cover and refrigerate. Melt butter in a skillet and sauté onion until tender; add mushrooms and spinach and cook until spinach wilts. Blend pepper into mixture. Cut away 2 ounces of flounder and reserve for sauce. Divide remaining flounder into 4 equal pieces; place each piece on one side of a pastry sheet and cover with a portion of the spinach mixture. Fold pastry over fish. Beat egg and brush over pastry seams to seal. Prick pastry and place each one on a greased baking sheet. Bake at 375 degrees for about 20 to 25 minutes or until golden brown. Serve with Dill Sauce (recipe below). Serves 4.

Dill Sauce:

4 tablespoons butter	1 tablespoon flour
1 shallot, finely diced	½ pint heavy cream
2 ounces flounder (reserved from above recipe)	1 tablespoon dried dill
	1 teaspoon white pepper

Melt butter in small skillet and sauté shallot and flounder until fish flakes. Add flour and blend into mixture until smooth. Add cream and bring to a boil, then add dill and pepper and stir until incorporated.

THE CITY TAVERN'S HOT BUTTERED RUM

5 ounces apple cider	1½ ounces dark rum
1 tablespoon butter	1 cinnamon stick

In a small saucepan heat apple cider and butter until the butter melts; add rum and cinnamon stick. Serves 1.

THE ANCHOR INN
Wrightstown

THE ANCHOR INN   An old menu from The Anchor Inn lists a handful of entrées, among them Chicken Giblet Stew and something called Creamed Frizzled Beef on Toast. It is doubtful that today's diners would be willing to give such oddities a try. Contemporary tastes run more toward Chateaubriand, Veal Oscar, Bouillabaisse or Pork Tenderloin Sauerbraten.

Some locals believe that the original Anchor Tavern was built by Joseph Hampton in 1724, which would make it the oldest continuously operating inn in Bucks County. However, county historians believe its origins were somewhat later. They cite documents showing that Joseph's son, Benjamin Hampton, purchased the land at the crossroads of Durham Road and the Richboro–Pineville Turnpike in 1767. In any case, five years thereafter, Benjamin applied for a liquor license for his Anchor Tavern. It is now surmised that his Quaker conscience balked at selling spirits, for he let the license expire in 1770 and sold the tavern in 1773.

The original plastered stone building had cooking and eating facilities downstairs and lodging upstairs. The second-floor guest rooms (now offices and dining rooms for private parties) were for the carriage trade. The third-story economy rooms under the eaves had small floor-level windows through which the guest could look only by lying on his stomach.

The four rooms on the first floor have been combined into a single spacious dining room with just two old wooden mantels to remind present-day diners of the tavern as it once was. A new wing features a comfortable lounge and dining terrace.

Cuisine is canted toward the Continental and includes specialties from various countries. There is a great deal of elegant tableside cooking, and the wine list is exemplary.

Even diet-conscious diners will find several suitable offerings. Fresh Fruit with Sorbet, listed as a starter, could be either an appetizer or dessert. There are several excellent salads, including Hot Spinach Salad. Broiled Lamb Chops, Medallions of Veal with Lime and Capers or Poached Salmon (light on the Béarnaise Sauce) are mouth-watering entrée selections.—c.w.

The Anchor Inn is located at the intersection of routes 232 and 413 in Wrightstown. Lunch is served from 11:30 a.m. until 2:30 p.m., Monday through Friday. Dinner is served from 5:30 p.m. until 9:00 p.m., Monday through Thursday, and from 5:30 p.m. until 11:00 p.m., Friday and Saturday. Sunday brunch is served from noon until 3:00 p.m. and dinner from 3:00 p.m. until 8:00 p.m. For reservations (recommended) call (215) 598-7171.

THE ANCHOR INN'S BOUILLABAISSE

4 tablespoons olive oil
1 garlic clove, crushed
2 large or 3 medium onions, julienned
4 leeks, well washed and julienned
1 tablespoon whole black peppercorns, crushed
1 bay leaf
7 cups hot fish stock (home-made, or use bottled clam juice as a substitute)
½ teaspoon saffron
pinch of thyme
½ teaspoon fennel
2 tablespoons chopped fresh parsley

3 tomatoes, peeled, seeded and cubed
1 cup dry white wine
2 potatoes, peeled and diced
1½ pounds non-flakey fish (fresh swordfish, tuna, salmon, monkfish)
6 shrimp, shelled
6 clams, scrubbed
6 mussels, scrubbed
1 live lobster, killed, split and cleaned
2 tablespoons Pernod
salt and pepper to taste

In a large saucepan, heat oil. Add garlic, onions and leeks, and sauté, stirring occasionally, until soft and translucent. Add crushed peppercorns and bay leaf and sauté 2 minutes. Add hot fish stock, saffron, thyme, fennel, parsley, tomatoes and white wine. Bring to a boil, then turn down heat and simmer 15 minutes. Add potatoes and simmer until tender, about 15 minutes. Meanwhile, trim and cut fish into large chunks. Place all seafood into another large saucepan. Pour in soup mixture and Pernod, bring to a boil and simmer until clams and mussels open and until all seafood is cooked. Adjust seasoning with salt and pepper. Serves 4 to 6.

THE ANCHOR INN'S PORK TENDERLOIN SAUERBRATEN

2 cups cold water
1 cup red wine vinegar
1 cup Burgundy
1 cup finely diced onion
1 cup peeled and finely
   diced carrot
1 cup finely diced celery
4 tablespoons brown sugar
1 garlic clove, chopped
2 tablespoons salt
1 bay leaf

½ teaspoon peppercorns,
   crushed
2 whole cloves
½ teaspoon ground ginger
6 pork tenderloins, totaling
   3 to 4 pounds
salt and pepper to taste
1 cup flour
2½ cups sweet butter
1½ cups mushrooms, sliced
1½ cups Madeira

Make a marinade by mixing water, vinegar, Burgundy, diced vegetables, sugar, garlic and spices in a large stainless steel bowl. Trim fat from pork tenderloin and place it into the bowl, covering all surfaces with the marinade. Refrigerate overnight, occasionally turning the meat in the marinade. Remove meat from marinade and pat dry. Pour marinade into a large saucepan and bring to a boil. Reduce by one-third and strain out vegetables. Meanwhile, slice the meat into ¼-inch slices and pound gently. Season meat slices with salt and pepper and flour lightly. Melt butter in a large skillet. Sauté meat slices on both sides until brown. Add mushrooms, reduced marinade and Madeira. Simmer for 5 to 8 minutes. Correct seasoning with salt and pepper. Serves 4 to 6.

DOYLESTOWN INN
Doylestown

DOYLESTOWN INN   If you're in the mood for an eclectic old inn where you can get a fudge sundae for breakfast or scrambled eggs for supper, the Doylestown Inn is the spot. It's a homey gathering place where locals stop for meals and munchies, or just to have a drink and swap gossip.

The inn occupies what were originally three buildings in the center of the Bucks County seat. One was a hattery, one was a grocery store and the third was an oyster house and saloon. The pier mirror in the front dining room is a souvenir from the oyster-house era, but otherwise, the inn has been redone several times.

In 1871, the inn became the Pollock Hotel, where General Hap Arnold debriefed Colonel Charles A. Lindbergh after the aviator had observed the German Air Force in the 1930s, and also where Oscar Hammerstein is reputed to have written some of his famous melodies. James Michener, who grew up in Doylestown, was a frequent guest, and Pearl Buck, Henry Fonda and Dorothy Parker are known to have visited.

Still, by the late 1970s, the hotel closed down and appeared to be doomed. In 1982, it was rescued by Dennis Sakelson and Nicholas Adams, who have succeeded in making it a local watering hole again.

The two adjoining dining rooms are comfortable, casual spaces with an ever-changing display of works by area artists on the walls. The busy Publick Tavern features a long bar and cozy booths. The Jug in the Wall downstairs, which takes its name from a constantly running spring tapped by an old pottery jug embedded in the masonry, has the air of a sidewalk café brought indoors.

Dennis and Nick willingly serve anything available, at any time of day or evening, in any of the dining rooms or lounges. I opted for traditional dinner selections, starting with Potato Skins, a crunchy appetizer with assorted toppings. The Walnut Chicken accompanied by lightly sautéed snowpeas was excellent, but it was a tough choice between that and one of the Oriental Stir Fry entrées. For dessert, I dug happily into Brownies à la James Beard, a rich house-special brownie topped with a double dip of vanilla ice cream, chocolate sauce and whipped cream.

For dieters with more willpower than I, the Doylestown Inn serves several small fresh vegetable salads, plus clams on the half-shell, steamed littlenecks and a fish of the day, which may be ordered broiled.—c.w.

The Doylestown Inn is located at 18 West State Street in Doylestown. Breakfast is served from 7:00 a.m. until 10:30 a.m., Monday through Saturday, and from 7:00 a.m. until 1:00 p.m. on Sunday. Lunch is served from 11:30 a.m. until 2:30 p.m., Monday through Saturday. Dinner is served from 5:00 p.m. until 11:00 p.m., Monday through Saturday, and from 4:00 p.m. until 11:00 p.m. on Sunday. For reservations (recommended) call (215) 345-6610.

DOYLESTOWN INN'S ORIENTAL BEEF STIR FRY

1 to 1½ pounds flank steak
½ cup soy sauce
½ cup olive oil
½ cup dry sherry
1 tablespoon minced garlic
2 tablespoons peanut oil
2 teaspoons cornstarch
¼ cup soy sauce
½ cup dry sherry
¼ teaspoon cayenne (optional)

1 teaspoon fresh ginger, peeled and grated
½ cup of any of the following sliced fresh vegetables (a combination of two or three is suitable): mushrooms, zucchini, bok choy, green or red peppers, onion or any other favorite

Chill the flank steak in the freezer until firm, then slice thinly on the bias. Make marinade of soy sauce, olive oil, sherry and garlic. Pour over sliced meat and allow to marinate in refrigerator overnight. Heat peanut oil in a large skillet or wok over medium-high heat. Remove meat from marinade with a slotted spoon and sauté in oil until browned, stirring frequently. Meanwhile, mix cornstarch with soy sauce, sherry and cayenne. Stir ginger and vegetables into meat and continue sautéing, stirring frequently, until vegetables are cooked

71

but still crisp. Stir in soy sauce mixture and continue sautéing until sauce thickens and mixture is heated through. Serve with rice. Serves 4 to 6.

DOYLESTOWN INN'S BROWNIES

1 pound butter-margarine blend	4 cups sugar
	8 eggs
16 ounces semisweet chocolate	2 cups flour
	1 cup chopped walnut meats

Preheat oven to 350 degrees. Melt butter-margarine blend and chocolate in the top of a double boiler over hot water. Pour into a mixing bowl and stir in sugar. Add eggs, two at a time. Stir in flour and then walnut meats. Pour into a lightly greased 12x7x2-inch pan and bake for 30 minutes. Yields 8 to 12 brownies.

DOYLESTOWN INN'S WALNUT CHICKEN

1 8-ounce chicken breast, skinned and boned	1 cup chicken or veal stock
	¼ cup brandy
3 tablespoons chopped walnut meats	½ cup heavy cream
	1 tablespoon sweet butter

Press the rib side of the chicken breast into chopped walnut meats and set aside. In a small saucepan, boil stock until reduced to ½ cup. Remove from heat, pour in brandy and ignite to flame off alcohol. Reduce heat to medium, return saucepan to stove and reduce liquid by half. Stir in cream. Continue cooking, stirring occasionally, until reduced by half again. Meanwhile, melt butter in a small skillet over medium-high heat. Place chicken breast in the butter, nut side down, and sauté until the meat begins to turn white around the edges. Turn chicken breast over and reduce heat. Continue sautéeing until cooked through, about 5 minutes. Place chicken, nut side up, on a plate and spoon sauce over it. Serves 1.

BLACK BASS HOTEL
Lumberville

BLACK BASS HOTEL   Adlai Stevenson's favorite table was a tiny two-seater overlooking the Delaware River. Jack Cassidy and his brood always sat at a big round table. A young John F. Kennedy offered to buy an etching depicting a U.S. Senate session, circa 1850, right off the wall of the Jackson Room. There was once even a reservation for Queen Elizabeth and Princess Margaret, but the Princess got married instead and the royal tour of America was canceled.

In spite of this impressive guest list, the Black Bass, which was built in the 1740s as a fortified haven for colonial travelers, is the rare old eastern Pennsylvania inn that does not claim George Washington as an overnight guest. In truth, the Revolutionary-era innkeeper was loyal to the Crown and wouldn't put Washington up.

The inn was nearly a century old when a barge canal was built a few steps west of the Delaware River. It accommodated the canal diggers and for decades afterward played host to both bargemen and passengers.

Today Bucks County is awash with quaint inns, but in 1949, when Herbert Ward refurbished the Black Bass and filled it with antique furniture, such hotels were not in vogue in this country. Ward turned this American inn into an approximation of a small European hotel. He installed a pewter bar salvaged from the original Maxim's of Paris, displayed his vast collection of English royalty commemorative pieces, and began hanging old railroad signal lanterns, pierced tin lamps, double-arm oil lamps, and old wrought iron fixtures in what is believed to be the oldest room in the building.

It was in this Lantern Room that I dug into a late winter lunch. A small loaf of hot Nut Bread on a scarred board and a heap of cinnamon-scented Muffins in a basket were accompanied by a ramekin of sweet butter. I tried two salads, one with an excellent House Dressing of homemade mayonnaise spiked with Dijon mustard and horseradish, and one with an even better Roquefort Dressing.

How do you top two salads but with samplings of three popular seafood entrées? I tasted the New England Lobster

Pie, subtly sauced and topped with chives; Charleston Meeting Street Crabmeat in a light white sauce sprinkled with cheese; and Roast Scallops with Pistachio & Cognac Butter, delicately flavored yet satisfyingly rich. The Black Bass couples each entrée with homemade pasta or a combination of long-grain and wild rice. For dessert, both the Deep Dish Apple Pie and the Rum Cream Pie are house specialties.

The Black Bass Hotel is perhaps the prototype for the many wonderful inns that have been created from old buildings, and it still remains one of Bucks County's most popular.—c.w.

The Black Bass Hotel is located on Route 32 in Lumberville. Lunch is served from noon until 2:30 p.m. and dinner from 5:30 p.m. until 9:00 p.m., Monday through Saturday. Sunday brunch is served from 11:00 a.m. until 3:00 p.m., and Sunday dinner is from 4:00 p.m. until 8:00 p.m. For reservations (required) call (215) 297-5770.

BLACK BASS HOTEL'S MUFFINS

1½ cups white flour
½ cup whole wheat flour
1½ teaspoons baking
    powder
pinch of salt
4 tablespoons brown sugar
3 tablespoons white sugar

¼ teaspoon cinnamon
¼ teaspoon nutmeg
5 tablespoons sweet butter
1 cup pumpkin purée,
    canned or homemade
2 eggs
milk

Preheat oven to 400 degrees. Sift all the dry ingredients into a mixing bowl. Cut butter into small pieces and blend into the dry ingredients with a pastry blender until mixture reaches a crumbly texture. Stir in pumpkin, eggs and sufficient milk to moisten batter. Spoon into greased muffin tins, filling each cup one-third full. Bake 7 to 10 minutes. Yields 24 muffins.

BLACK BASS HOTEL'S DEEP DISH APPLE PIE

2 pounds McIntosh apples
4 tablespoons dry white
  wine
½ cup brown sugar
1 cup seedless raisins
pinch each of cloves, cinnamon and nutmeg

12 ounces pie dough, homemade or packaged
1 egg
1 tablespoon water

Preheat oven to 425 degrees. Peel, core and coarsely chop apples. Combine chopped apples, wine, sugar, raisins and spices. Spoon into a 1½-inch-deep, 9-inch pie dish. Roll out dough and top apple mixture with crust, patting edges firmly and making two slits in the center to allow steam to escape. Lightly beat egg with 1 tablespoon water. With a pastry brush, paint this egg wash over top of pie. Bake 20 to 25 minutes, until crust is golden brown. Yields one 9-inch deep-dish pie.

BLACK BASS HOTEL'S ROQUEFORT DRESSING

1 cup olive oil
½ cup red wine vinegar
1 teaspoon chopped fresh
  parsley
½ teaspoon dry English
  mustard

3 tablespoons soy sauce
1 teaspoon finely chopped
  shallots
¼ to ½ pound Roquefort
  cheese

Mix the olive oil, vinegar, parsley, mustard, soy sauce and shallots until smooth. Crumble cheese into dressing and mix lightly. Serves 12.

DONZES RED LION INN
Quakertown

DONZES RED LION INN

Early in September 1777, when it became evident that the British were about to occupy Philadelphia, the Continental Congress decreed that stores and matériel ought to be moved lest they fall into enemy hands. Among the objects to be safeguarded were all of the city's bells and chimes, which could be melted down and cast into bullets.

So began the odyssey of at least a dozen bells, which were removed secretly and loaded into Pennsylvania Dutch farmers' wagons for the sixty-five-mile journey to Northampton Town (now Allentown). The trip took eight days, including a tactical detour that may have taken the seven-hundred-wagon convoy, guarded by two hundred troops, as far afield as Trenton.

On the night of September 23, the State House Bell—one of the largest—was hidden behind a small stone house in Quakertown. The officers crossed the road to spend the night at the Stage Coach Inn, while the men under their command bedded down in stables and sheds.

The State House Bell is now known as the Liberty Bell. The Stage Coach Inn has become Donzés Red Lion Inn, and the small stone house is now Liberty Hall, which is notable both historically and architecturally.

The past and the present have come together in the person of Thomas J. Donzé, who was a prime mover in the recent restoration of Liberty Hall and who with his wife, Evelyn, runs the old inn. Donzés Red Lion Inn is an unpretentious place. Its congenial bar is a favorite local pub, and its spacious, casual dining rooms are popular with families. Some tables have seats that were once church pews, and others are eclectically ringed by chairs of various styles. Antique plates, old glass and photographs of Quakertown in earlier years add a patina to the comfortable old-fashioned atmosphere.

The menu is suffused with old standbys—some local favorites like the Poorman's Dinner, a medley of beef and shrimp, and other widely loved staples like Veal Parmigiana, Baked Stuffed Shrimp or the Mariner's Combination Seafood Platter.

All are served in generous portions. There are three different mushroom appetizers, always a soup and a potato of the day and desserts from Evelyn Donzé's repertoire.

Sautéed Mushrooms or a Fresh Fruit Cup would suit a dieter as a starter, followed by Chopped Broiled Sirloin Steak, Broiled Deep Sea Scallops or Sea and Land, which enables the diner to couple steak with a choice of shrimp, scallops or flounder.—c.w.

Donzés Red Lion Inn is located at Broad and Main streets in Quakertown. Lunch is served from 11:30 a.m. until 2:30 p.m., Tuesday through Saturday. Dinner is served from 4:30 p.m. until 9:00 p.m., Wednesday and Thursday; from 4:30 p.m. until 10:00 p.m., Friday and Saturday; and from 1:30 p.m. until 8:00 p.m. on Sunday. Sunday breakfast is served from 8:00 a.m. until noon. For reservations (requested for groups of 8 or more) call (215) 536-5283.

DONZES RED LION INN'S STRAWBERRY CHEESECAKE

¼ cup sweet butter
1½ cups graham cracker
   crumbs, finely crushed
¼ cup sugar
2 8-ounce packages cream
   cheese at room
   temperature
1 cup sugar
1½ tablespoons flour

2 teaspoons grated orange
   rind
⅛ teaspoon salt
1 teaspoon vanilla extract
3 large eggs
2 tablespoons sour cream
1 pint fresh strawberries
¼ cup currant jelly
1 teaspoon water

In a medium-size skillet over low heat, melt butter. Stir in graham cracker crumbs and ¼ cup sugar. Using the back of a spoon, firmly press the crumb mixture over the bottom and 1½ inches up the rim of an 8-inch springform pan; set aside. Preheat oven to 550 degrees. In a medium bowl, beat together cream cheese and 1 cup sugar. Beat in flour, orange rind, salt and vanilla. Beat in eggs, one at a time, and then the sour cream. Pour into the prepared springform pan. Bake at 550 degrees for five minutes. Reduce temperature to 200 degrees

79

and continue baking for 25 to 30 minutes, or until a knife inserted 2 inches from the edge of the pan comes out clean. Remove from oven and cool completely in the pan. Meanwhile, hull strawberries and cut in half. Over low heat, stir together currant jelly and water in a small saucepan until jelly melts; set aside. Gently move a small metal spatula up and down around the rim of the springform pan. Carefully remove the rim. Arrange strawberries, cut side down, in a pleasing pattern over the top of the cake. Spoon jelly over strawberries. Refrigerate until serving. Yields 1 cheesecake.

DONZES RED LION INN'S RATATOUILLE

½ cup salad oil
1 medium onion, chopped
1 garlic clove, crushed
½ cup green pepper, seeded
   and coarsely chopped
½ cup sweet red pepper,
   seeded and coarsely
   chopped
1 20-ounce can whole
   tomatoes

2 large zucchini, scrubbed
   and sliced
1 small eggplant, peeled
   and cubed
2 teaspoons salt (or to taste)
¼ teaspoon pepper
1 bay leaf
1 teaspoon oregano
pinch of thyme

In a medium saucepan over medium heat, heat oil and sauté onion, garlic and peppers until soft. Add juice from tomatoes and simmer for 10 minutes. Add tomatoes, zucchini, eggplant and seasonings. Continue simmering, stirring occasionally, until vegetables are tender, about 15 minutes. Serves 6 to 8.

COVENTRY FORGE INN
Coventryville

COVENTRY FORGE INN

There was a time, not long ago, when it was difficult to get a sophisticated meal anywhere between New York and San Francisco. One of the first restaurants to fill that gap was the Coventry Forge Inn, an early outpost of French cuisine in the Pennsylvania countryside.

The inn was created by E. Wallis Callahan in the house where he grew up. The core is a small log structure built in 1717 and added to over the years. It was a drovers' inn from 1750 to 1818 and a private home before and after. Wallie Callahan's mother bought it in 1937 and was instrumental in helping her son turn it into one of the finest restaurants in the state.

Cozy areas like the bar, with its large fireplace, make dining at Coventry Forge an intimate experience. Perhaps the most intimate room of all is the Pine Room, a tiny wood-paneled chamber of such exquisite proportions that New York's Metropolitan Museum sought to dismantle it and display it as part of their American collection.

For the Coventry Forge Inn's opening day on May 30, 1954, Wallie Callahan opted for a *table d'hôte* dinner of dishes he believed would be delicious but not too daring. He felt that customers of the conservative 1950s might be scared away by a meal that was too French or too fancy. The dinner, which cost three dollars, started with Shrimp Rémoulade and ended with Strawberry Shortcake. The entrée was Sautéed Chicken Coventry Forge, which, simple though it now seems, has remained a favorite over the years.

Today, staples such as Soupe à l'Oignon Gratinée, Caneton à l'Orange and Crême Caramel Réversée—all done with particular panache—share the bill of fare with specials. In the spring, Callahan's traditional Baked Shad with Roe Filling is a seasonal treat.

Accompanying the fine fare are offerings from the inn's extensive wine cellar. Callahan, whose passion is wine, is not only an award-winning chef, but a card-carrying oenophile. He is a member of both Les Amis de Bordeaux and Les Chevaliers du Tastevin.

Because of the care with which the Coventry Forge Inn

handles simple dishes, the restaurant is a good bet for weight-watchers, who may select simple broiled fish, meat or poultry grilled to perfection.—c.w.

The Coventry Forge Inn is located in Coventryville, south of Pottstown. Dinner is served from 5:30 p.m. until 9:00 p.m., Tuesday through Friday (and also on Monday during daylight saving time), and from 5:00 p.m. until 10:00 p.m. on Saturday. For reservations (required) call (215) 469-6222.

COVENTRY FORGE INN'S BAKED SHAD WITH ROE FILLING

roe from 1 medium shad
1 tablespoon chopped shallots
3 slices white bread (crusts removed), coarsely diced
3 tablespoons chopped fresh parsley

1½ sticks sweet butter, melted
salt and pepper to taste
tarragon to taste
lemon slices

Preheat oven to 350 degrees. Poach the roe in salted water for about 5 minutes, taking care not to overcook. Remove roe from sac and work through a coarse sieve into a bowl containing shallots, bread, parsley and butter. Mix thoroughly and add salt, pepper and tarragon. Spread mixture on one shad fillet and top with second fillet. Place fish on a buttered gratin dish and bake for about 20 minutes. Garnish with lemon slices. Serves 4 to 6.

COVENTRY FORGE INN'S SAUTEED CHICKEN COVENTRY FORGE

flour
salt and pepper to taste
pinch of monosodium glutamate (optional)
thighs, legs and halved breast of one 2- to 3-pound broiling or frying chicken

3 tablespoons sweet butter
½ cup dry white wine
2 tablespoons sliced almonds
fresh parsley or watercress

83

Put the flour, salt, pepper and optional monosodium gluta-mate into a paper bag and add chicken pieces, shaking to coat. In a heavy skillet, melt 2 tablespoons butter and add the chicken. Cook uncovered over low heat, 10 minutes on each side. Pour wine over chicken, cover and continue cooking for another 5 minutes. Meanwhile, melt 1 tablespoon butter in a small skillet and lightly brown almonds in butter, stirring frequently to prevent burning. Place chicken on a serving plate. Pour pan gravy and almonds (with butter) over chicken. Garnish with parsley or watercress. Serves 2 to 3.

COVENTRY FORGE INN'S GRAND MARNIER SOUFFLE

4 tablespoons unsalted butter	4 tablespoons Grand Marnier liqueur
2 tablespoons flour	pinch of salt
1 cup heavy cream	½ teaspoon cream of tartar
4 egg yolks	butter and sugar for soufflé mold
5 tablespoons sugar	
6 egg whites	

Preheat oven to 400 degrees. In a small saucepan, melt butter and stir in flour. Stir in cream and continue cooking until thickened. Beat egg yolks with 4 tablespoons sugar until thick and lemon-colored. Stir in cream mixture and Grand Marnier. Beat 6 egg whites with salt and cream of tartar until frothy. Add 1 tablespoon sugar and continue beating until stiff but not dry. Beat one-fourth of the egg-white mixture into the yolk mixture, then carefully fold in remaining egg-white mix-ture. Pour into a buttered, sugared 6-cup soufflé mold. Place mold in a pan of hot water and bake for 15 to 20 minutes until puffed and lightly golden. Serve immediately. Serves 4.

HOAR HOUSE
Lancaster

HOAR HOUSE

My friends were certain they'd misunderstood when I told them I'd been to the Hoar House. But the real misunderstanding occurred in 1873, when the good people of Lancaster decided to build a first-class hotel. Originally, the hotel was to bear the name of Lancaster's controversial politician, Thaddeus Stevens. A noted abolitionist, Stevens was the catalyst for Lincoln's Emancipation Proclamation.

When the hotel building fund fell short, additional stocks were offered with the incentive that the hotel would now be named after the person who purchased the largest block of stock. When the sales of stock were tallied, it developed that a prominent coal and ice dealer, Jacob Hoar, had bought the most. This put the fund raisers in a pickle, as the townspeople were already trying to rid their community of an abundance of actual whorehouses. Hence, a scarlet-faced spokesman announced that the hotel would be named the Stevens House after all.

Time, courage and a sense of humor can sometimes rectify injustice. Today, because an extraordinary restaurant believes that Jacob Hoar has waited long enough for his proper recognition, the establishment has been renamed the Hoar House.

Claire Walter and I entered this den of gastronomical delight with barely restrained giggles, which erupted the moment we saw the display of art and mirrors on the ceiling. A tuxedoed waiter ceremoniously ushered us toward a candlelit table in a Victorian-style room swathed in red velvet. Discreetly, we peeped into private lace-curtained alcoves suggestive of clandestine liaisons.

Although the restaurant takes a tongue-in-cheek attitude towards décor, their Continental-style cuisine is definitely a serious affair. Beginning our meal with their distinctly flavored Turtle Soup, Claire and I savored each sip as though tasting an exquisite wine. Changing our rhythm, we began to ooh over Clams Casino with a green pepper–pimento butter. Baroque music wafted in with their Scallops Primavera, which were as scandalously delicious as they were low in calories. Our next entrée was called Tournedos Dubois, and I was completely seduced by the voluptuous sauce flavored with the unlikely combination of blueberries and raspberry vinegar.

Desserts at Hoar House are pure decadent downfall, but we remained virtuous, agreeing that experiencing this restaurant was dessert in itself.

Hoar House is located at 10 South Prince Street in Lancaster. Dinner is served from 5:00 p.m. until 11:00 p.m., Tuesday through Saturday. Sunday dinner is served from 11:00 a.m. until 9:00 p.m. For reservations (required) call (717) 397-0110.

HOAR HOUSE'S TOURNEDOS DUBOIS

8 4-ounce tenderloin tournedos
4 tablespoons clarified butter
4 shallots, chopped
4 garlic cloves, finely chopped
¼ pound fresh mushrooms, quartered
2 medium tomatoes, diced

4 tablespoons peppercorns, ground
½ cup brandy
¼ cup raspberry vinegar
1 pint Brown Sauce (see index)
½ cup fresh or frozen blueberries
salt and pepper to taste

In a large skillet, sauté beef in butter until it reaches desired doneness; remove and set aside. Drain butter from skillet; add shallots, garlic, mushrooms, tomatoes, peppercorns, brandy and raspberry vinegar. Simmer for a few moments. Add Brown Sauce, blueberries, salt and pepper and stir until heated through. Reheat beef and serve covered with sauce. Serves 4.

HOAR HOUSE'S TURTLE SOUP

water to cover turtle, about 1 gallon

1 cup tomato purée
1 cup dry sherry

1 4- to 5-pound whole turtle, fresh or frozen
1 medium onion, diced
2 large green peppers, diced
2 celery stalks, diced
4 garlic cloves, chopped
½ pound butter
⅓ cup all-purpose flour
1 lemon, halved
2 bay leaves
½ teaspoon oregano
½ teaspoon thyme
1 ounce seafood seasoning
¼ cup lobster base
4 hard-boiled eggs
¼ pound fresh spinach

In enough water to cover, cook the whole turtle for 2 to 3 hours. Turtle is ready when meat is tender. Strain the juices and save stock. Remove the meat from the shell and set aside to cool. Discard the shell and bones. Sauté onions, peppers, celery and garlic in butter until soft. Slowly add flour and cook for 2 minutes, stirring constantly. Add the turtle stock, tomato purée, dry sherry, lemon, seasonings and lobster base. Reduce heat to a simmer. Finely chop the turtle meat, eggs and spinach. After the soup has simmered for 1 hour, add turtle meat, eggs and spinach. Serves 8 to 10.

HOAR HOUSE'S SCALLOPS PRIMAVERA

1 pound fresh sea scallops
½ cup flour
4 tablespoons clarified butter
4 tablespoons butter
2 garlic cloves, chopped
1 zucchini, julienned
1 carrot, julienned
4 large fresh mushrooms, sliced
¼ cup white wine
½ cup whipping cream
¼ cup tomato sauce
¼ cup Parmesan cheese
salt and pepper to taste

Dredge scallops in flour, and sauté in clarified butter until half done. Remove scallops. Drain grease from pan; add butter, garlic, julienned vegetables, mushrooms and white wine. Stir, reduce heat and add cream and tomato sauce. Simmer for a few moments. Roll scallops in flour again and add to mixture. Add cheese, salt and pepper. Serves 4.

GROFF'S FARM RESTAURANT
Mount Joy

**GROFF'S FARM
RESTAURANT**

The morning that Claire and I visited Groff's Farm, our refreshment began where their dinner guests' normally ends—in the wine cellar. In spite of the early hour, Betty Groff invited us to sample a bit of her homemade wine, an invitation she and her husband, Abe, usually extend to their guests at evening's end.

As we sipped a mildly sweet apple wine, we toured the cellar of this sturdy stone farmhouse. The cellar walls, insulated with a straw-mud cement laced with horsehair, were lined with rows of Betty's canned vegetables, jams and pickles. Hung from the ceiling or drying in bins were herbs and fruits, reminding us that this country-fresh style of cooking is an unhurried, ongoing process.

Back upstairs in the kitchen, we watched our meal being prepared—my first chance to observe Pennsylvania Dutch cooking methods. Then we moved to the dining room, where we began, as I always vowed I would as a child, with dessert! Betty doesn't believe that people should miss dessert because they are too full from their main course. It was turning into quite a morning—first Apple Wine, now Cracker Pudding and, what else? Shoo Fly Pie, of course!

Eager to see the other rooms, we toured between courses. We learned that when the McFarland family built this home in 1756, they had to pay a "light tax"—a tax on nine windows, paid to England for the privilege of using light! Perhaps next time I won't be so quick to gripe about paying taxes.

Our well-lit dining room was decorated in its original pale aqua, so I was surprised to see bright colors, typical of the Pennsylvania Dutch, in the other rooms. I had thought that the Mennonites were a somber people, but I discovered that their décor is as friendly as they are.

The unmistakable perfume of ham, cured by Betty's father, summoned us back to our table, where we also enjoyed Betty's famous Chicken Stoltzfus. We devoured these savory treats along with a green salad with a creamy, sweet-and-sour Hot Bacon Dressing and freshly baked bread. This fabulous feast concluded a homespun experience that will forever stand out among my nostalgic thoughts of Pennsylvania.

Groff's Farm Restaurant is located on Pinkerton Road in Mount Joy. Lunch is served from 11:30 a.m. until 1:30 p.m., Tuesday through Saturday, and from 11:30 a.m. until 2:30 p.m. on Sunday. Dinner seatings are at 5:00 p.m. and 7:30 p.m., Tuesday through Saturday. Wine may be brought. For reservations (required) call (717) 653-2048.

GROFF'S FARM RESTAURANT'S CHICKEN STOLTZFUS

1 5-pound roasting chicken, giblets removed
1½ quarts water
1 tablespoon salt
⅓ teaspoon pepper
pinch of saffron
1½ sticks butter
12 tablespoons flour
1 cup half and half
¼ cup finely chopped fresh parsley or ⅛ cup dried parsley
Pastry Squares (recipe below)
parsley

Place chicken in a 6-quart pot and add water, salt, pepper and saffron; bring to a boil. Reduce heat and simmer, partially covered, for 1 hour. Remove chicken and let cool. Debone chicken, remove skin and cut meat into bite-sized pieces. Strain the stock and reduce it to 4 cups. Melt butter in original pot and stir in flour to make a roux. Cook until bubbling, then add stock and cream, stirring constantly until sauce reaches a boil. Simmer until thickened and smooth, then add chicken and parsley. Serve over warm Pastry Squares, garnished with additional parsley. Serves 6.

Pastry Squares:
½ cup lard or vegetable shortening
½ cup butter
3 cups all-purpose flour
1 teaspoon salt
about ½ cup ice water

Cut the lard and butter into the flour with two knives or a pastry blender until it forms coarse crumbs. Sprinkle ice water over the crumbs with one hand while tossing them lightly with the other. Use only enough water to hold the dough together. Press the dough into a ball and turn it out onto a lightly floured surface. Divide into 2 or 3 parts. Roll each part to ⅛ inch thick. Cut dough into 1-inch squares and bake on ungreased cookie sheets in a preheated 350-degree oven for 12 to 15 minutes, until light brown.

GROFF'S FARM RESTAURANT'S HOT BACON DRESSING

¼ pound bacon
1 tablespoon cornstarch
¾ teaspoon salt
1½ tablespoons sugar

1 slightly beaten egg
3 scant tablespoons cider vinegar
1 cup milk

Fry bacon in a skillet until crisp, and drain on paper towels. In a small bowl combine the dry ingredients. Whisk in egg and stir until smooth. Slowly whisk in vinegar. Blend milk with egg mixture and slowly add it to the bacon fat in the skillet over medium heat, stirring constantly. Bring to boil for 1 minute, whisking constantly. Crumble the bacon and add half to the dressing, reserving remainder for garnishing the salad. This dressing may also be served cold, or refrigerated and reheated at a later time. Yields 1¼ cups.

GROFF'S FARM RESTAURANT'S CRACKER PUDDING

1 quart milk
2 eggs, separated
⅔ cup sugar
2 cups broken saltines (not crumbs)

1 cup grated coconut
1 teaspoon vanilla

In a heavy 3-quart pot heat the milk until almost boiling. In a separate bowl beat egg yolks and sugar until frothy. Slowly add to hot milk. Reduce heat to medium. Crumble saltines into milk and stir constantly until boiling. Add coconut and stir until pudding bubbles thickly. Remove from heat and add vanilla. Beat egg whites until stiff and carefully fold into mixture. Serve warm or cold. Serves 6 to 8.

THE CAMERON ESTATE INN
Mount Joy

**THE CAMERON
ESTATE INN**

History makes no bones about President Ulysses S. Grant's favorite hobby—drinking. When Claire Walter and I dined at the Cameron Estate Inn, we learned that President Grant had indulged in that hobby in the very room in which we dined. The Federalist-style home, built in 1805 by Dr. John Watson (great-grandfather of President William McKinley), was purchased in 1872 by the infamous politician Simon Cameron, and Grant visited Cameron regularly. Betty and Abe Groff, who restored the mansion to its original European manor elegance, told us that one night Grant bet Cameron that he could drink him under the table. Not only did Grant lose the bet, but the servants had to remove the room's sliding door to use as a stretcher for the intoxicated president.

Not wanting to fall into that president's predicament, Claire and I cautiously ordered an Alexis Lichine rosé. We hadn't planned it, but our wine was exactly the color of the pink daisies decorating our pale green tablecloth. These colors complemented the décor of this gracious room, with its cabbage-rose wallpaper, cozy fireplace, and original herringbone-patterned cherrywood floors.

Deciding that it was time to put the skids on calorie consumption, I ordered their Fresh Fruit Salad (marinated in orange liqueur) with Poppy Seed Dressing, while Claire enjoyed a Monte Cristo Croissant. These dishes are typical of the New American Cuisine that I so heartily endorse, which marries French techniques to fresh American ingredients.

Next we sampled a Cauliflower Harlequin, prepared with ham, Swiss cheese and bread crumbs, along with their utterly wonderful Chicken Sauté "Simon Cameron." This dish, laced with capers, is whimsically named after Cameron because of his political capers. Four times a United States Senator, this self-made man was also the first Secretary of War during the Lincoln administration. Congress requested his resignation from this post when it was proved that he had showed favoritism in the letting of government contracts. However, political tides sometimes turn rather rapidly, and he was appointed

Ambassador to Russia that same year. Fifteen years later, he resigned from the senate so that his son, James Donald Cameron, might be elected in his place.

For dessert we discovered Bailey's Irish Cream Pie. This treat has a creamy texture, with a heavenly richness that is perfect with a cup of coffee.

After our meal, we wanted to see more of this home that is on the National Historic Register, so we trekked up the wide stairway to the third floor to take a peek at the bedrooms. Every room has beautiful handmade quilts that carry the room's motif. Some rooms are massive baronial suites with working fireplaces and period furnishings that complement the architectural detailing, while others are intimate dormer rooms. But each provides a tranquil atmosphere that I would be happy to call home for a weekend or so. And that's exactly what I plan to do the next time I'm in the area.

The Cameron Estate Inn is located on Donegal Springs Road in Mount Joy. Lunch is served from 11:30 a.m. until 2:00 p.m., daily. Dinner is served from 6:00 p.m. until 8:30 p.m., Monday through Thursday, and from 5:30 p.m. until 9:30 p.m., Friday and Saturday. Champagne brunch is served on Sunday during luncheon hours. For reservations (required) call (717) 653-1773.

THE CAMERON ESTATE INN'S CHICKEN SAUTE "SIMON CAMERON"

4 chicken breasts, deboned and skinned	4 artichoke hearts, halved
½ cup all-purpose flour	2 tablespoons brandy
4 tablespoons Garlic Butter (see index)	2 tablespoons capers
	4 lemon slices
8 fresh asparagus spears	chopped fresh parsley

Coat chicken with flour. Melt Garlic Butter in a skillet and brown chicken on both sides, cooking until firm. Remove chicken and add asparagus and artichoke hearts. Sauté lightly and carefully. Lower heat and place chicken back in skillet, covering asparagus and artichokes. Add brandy and capers and cook for 2 to 3 minutes. Remove and divide into 4 equal portions. Garnish with lemon slices and parsley. Serves 4.

THE CAMERON ESTATE INN'S
CAULIFLOWER HARLEQUIN

1 small head of cauliflower
2 tablespoons melted butter
¼ pound boiled ham or
  Canadian bacon, diced

2 hard-boiled eggs, diced
2 tablespoons fine bread
  crumbs
½ cup grated Swiss cheese

Parboil cauliflower. Drain and place in a 1½-quart buttered casserole. Pour melted butter over cauliflower and sprinkle with ham, eggs, bread crumbs and cheese. Bake at 375 degrees for 20 minutes. Serves 4.

THE CAMERON ESTATE INN'S BAILEY'S
IRISH CREAM PIE

4 egg whites
1 cup sugar
1 teaspoon vanilla
2 cups whipping cream
3½ tablespoons Bailey's
  Irish Cream liqueur

2 9-inch graham cracker
  crusts (see index)
shaved chocolate

Beat egg whites, gradually adding sugar and vanilla, until whites are stiff but still fluffy. Set aside. Whip cream until very stiff. Add liqueur to egg whites and gently fold mixture into whipped cream. Pour into pie shells. Cover tightly with plastic wrap and a layer of aluminum foil. Freeze until hard. Thaw about 10 minutes before serving and garnish with shaved chocolate. Yields 2 pies.

ALFRED'S VICTORIAN
Middletown

ALFRED'S VICTORIAN

The irregular outline of a roof sculpted with turrets and dormers suggests that a member of television's "Adams Family" could step out the front door of this marvelous old brownstone. Actually, this house, now on the National Register of Historic Places, isn't all that forbidding—it's just that it was built in 1888, at the height of the Gilded Age, when extravagance ran amok. Its original owner, Charles Raymond, may also have run a little amok financially, as the home went to the local bank to repay his creditors. It was later bought for $6,600 by Redsecker Young. Young sold it to Simon Cameron Young, who willed it to his daughters, Emman and Eliza. Alfred Pellegrini, the house's current owner, purchased the neglected mansion in 1970, one day before it was slated for demolition.

Once inside, you will be astounded by the opulence, from the leaded glass window transoms and the stained glass window lighting the stair tower to the hand-carved stairway and wainscoting. In the dining room, you'll see what appears to be floor-to-ceiling windows; they are actually massive doors that slide up into the ceiling.

One night, hearing footsteps behind those doors, Pellegrini called the police, who arrived with guns drawn, ready to confront the burglar. But when the doors were opened, no one was there. Apparently the intruder was not a burglar, but the spirit of Emman Young, who is thought to pace the floor pining for the lover that she was forbidden to marry.

We heard this tale as Pellegrini prepared our Caesar Salad tableside. The salad was delicious, as was my Steak Diane, also cooked at our table. I loved the contending flavors in their Vegetables Victorian. It didn't take long to understand why this restaurant was selected for America's top one hundred by *Cooking Magazine* and why Pellegrini's cooking has won him a coveted cache of awards.

After our feast, there was no way to slip in dessert, although watching Peaches Jubilee being flambéed at a neighboring table made me wish I had shown a little restraint. But restraint is a word that disappears from your vocabulary when you dine in this lavish setting.

98

Alfred's Victorian is located at 38 North Union Street in Middletown. Dinner is served from 5:00 p.m. until 10:00 p.m., Monday through Saturday, and from 3:00 p.m. until 10:00 p.m. on Sunday. For reservations (requested) call (717) 944-5373.

ALFRED'S VICTORIAN'S TOMATO MEAT SAUCE

1 tablespoon olive oil
3 tablespoons butter
1 garlic clove, minced
1 medium onion, chopped
4 sprigs fresh parsley, chopped
1 celery rib, chopped
2 ounces prosciutto, sliced and chopped
1 pound (combined) ground beef, pork and veal
3 to 4 fresh mushrooms, chopped
¼ cup dry red wine
pinch of rosemary

1 teaspoon dried marjoram
1½ teaspoons salt
1 teaspoon pepper
1 6-ounce can tomato paste
1 32-ounce can Italian plum tomatoes, chopped
3 to 4 fresh basil leaves, chopped, or 1 teaspoon dried basil
1 cup water
2 tablespoons butter
fresh grated nutmeg to taste
1½ pounds cooked pasta (or more)

Heat oil and butter in a large saucepan. Add garlic, onions, parsley and celery and sauté until onions are clear. Add prosciutto, ground meat, mushrooms, wine, rosemary, marjoram, salt and pepper. Sauté until meat is browned. Add tomato paste, tomatoes, basil and water. Cook about 1 hour on low heat. If too thick, add more water. Taste for salt. When sauce is nearly done, add butter and nutmeg. Serve over cooked pasta. Serves 8 to 10.

ALFRED'S VICTORIAN'S VEGETABLES VICTORIAN

½ cup olive oil
juice of 1 lemon
1 tablespoon wine vinegar
½ teaspoon salt
¼ teaspoon white pepper
dash of Tabasco sauce

1 pound of fresh vegetables, using any or all of the following: asparagus, cauliflower, broccoli, green beans

Place all ingredients except meat in a large skillet. Tilt skillet and stir ingredients into a sauce. Heat through. When hot, add meat and cook until done on both sides. Remove meat to warmed serving dishes. Taste sauce and adjust salt, then pour sauce over meat. Serves 4.

ALFRED'S VICTORIAN'S STEAK DIANE

4 tablespoons butter
juice of half a lemon
4 dashes Worcestershire
    sauce
3 to 4 dashes Tabasco sauce
½ teaspoon chopped fresh
    chives

salt and pepper to taste
2 ounces brandy
2 ounces sherry
4 8- to 10-ounce filets
    mignons, butterflied

Blend olive oil, lemon juice, wine vinegar, salt, pepper and Tabasco sauce in blender until combined; set aside. Place vegetables in steamer and steam until barely tender. Pour blended dressing over hot vegetables and serve immediately, or marinate vegetables in the dressisng for 15 to 30 minutes in the refrigerator and serve cold. Serves 4.

HOTEL HERSHEY
Hershey

HOTEL HERSHEY

Milton Hershey, who developed the chocolate bar that spawned today's food and entertainment empire, didn't like restaurants with pillars or corners. All diners, he felt, should be seated as if they were equally important. The Hotel Hershey's spacious dining room therefore has no pillars and just two walls—a straight back wall, and a curved wall of windows overlooking the exquisite formal gardens of this gracious hotel in America's chocolate capital.

The hotel is Mediterranean in style and grand in scale. It was built in 1933, based on plans inspired by a postcard of a European hostelry Milton Hershey admired. The dining room resembles a Spanish courtyard. Indirect lighting, white nappery and excellent acoustics give it an air of quiet elegance.

The menu changes daily, and the kitchen professes a "from-scratch" philosophy. The hotel smokes its own whitefish, salmon, trout, goose, duck and even pig—the latter for a Hawaiian luau, part of a series of international theme dinners featured in winter.

I knew that I would indulge in a chocolate dessert, but when I was presented with the dinner menu, I couldn't resist starting with Iced Chocolatetown Bisque—for where else in the world could I get chocolate soup? I also confess to tasting one of the evening's specials, a cold Minted Pear Soup. Both were smooth and rich.

After those calorie-laden starters, I selected a simple Broiled Fillet of Sole for my entrée. Hotel Hershey is also noted for excellent continental-style veal, and while I was tempted by the Veal Zurichoise, I couldn't sandwich that creamy entrée between two chocolate courses and still keep my belt buckled.

Many people eat at Hotel Hershey just for the desserts, and of all those treats, the Chocolate Sabayone Torte is the most popular. Card-carrying chocoholics descend on the hotel in hungry hordes for the Great American Chocolate Festival, which is held each February. For the rest of us, any day can be a chocolate festival with judicious selections from the menu.—C.W.

Hotel Hershey is located off Hersheypark Drive in Hershey. The hotel's dining room is open daily for breakfast from 7:00 a.m. until 9:30 a.m., for lunch from noon until 2:00 p.m., and for dinner from 6:00 until 9:00 p.m. Sunday brunch is served from 11:15 a.m. until 2:00 p.m. During the busy summer months, there are two dinner seatings, at 6:00 to 6:30 p.m. and at 8:30 to 9:00 p.m. For reservations (suggested) call (717) 533-2171, Extension 1.

HOTEL HERSHEY'S ICED CHOCOLATETOWN BISQUE

1 pint chocolate ice cream, softened
1 pint half and half
¼ cup Kahlúa
½ cup Amaretto
1 pint prepared instant chocolate pudding
1 cup sliced, toasted almonds

Combine ice cream, half and half, Kahlúa and Amaretto in a large bowl. Mix well. Blend in pudding and almonds. Freeze. Serves 10 to 12.

HOTEL HERSHEY'S CHOCOLATE SABAYONE TORTE

Classic Chocolate Cake:
¾ cup Hershey's Cocoa
⅔ cup boiling water
¾ cup butter or margarine, softened
2 cups sugar
1 teaspoon vanilla extract
2 eggs
2 cups unsifted cake flour
1¼ teaspoon baking soda
¼ teaspoon salt
¾ cup buttermilk or sour milk

In a small bowl, stir together cocoa and water until smooth; set aside. Cream butter or margarine with sugar and vanilla in a large mixer bowl. Blend in eggs. Combine flour, baking soda and salt. Add dry ingredients alternately with buttermilk or sour milk to the creamed mixture. Blend in the cocoa mixture. Pour batter into two greased and floured 9-inch cake pans. Bake in a 350-degree oven for 35 to 40 minutes, or until cake tester comes out clean. Cool 10 minutes; remove from pans. Cool completely on wire racks.

Filling:

5 egg yolks, lightly beaten	4¾ ounces Hershey's Sweet Chocolate, melted
¼ cup sugar	
⅓ cup sherry	1⅓ cups heavy cream
1 envelope unflavored gelatin	1 teaspoon unsifted confectioners' sugar
¼ cup cold water	½ teaspoon vanilla extract

Beat egg yolks, sugar and sherry in a bowl over warm water until mixture is lukewarm. Pour into large mixer bowl and beat until thick and lemon-colored, about 10 minutes. Meanwhile, soften gelatin in cold water and then heat over low heat, stirring until completely dissolved. Add melted chocolate to egg mixture. Add gelatin to egg-chocolate mixture, beating at low speed until cool. Whip cream with confectioners' sugar until thickened but not dry, adding vanilla at the end of the whipping process. Blend into chocolate mixture. Split each Classic Chocolate Cake layer in half crosswise to form four layers. Place one on plate and spread top with one-third of the filling (recipe above). Alternate remaining cake layers and filling, with fourth cake layer on top. Cover and chill until firm, about 3 to 4 hours. Frost with Chocolate Butter Cream (recipe below). Cover and chill until served. Yields 1 cake.

Chocolate Butter Cream:

3½ cups unsifted confectioners' sugar	½ cup milk
	1 teaspoon vanilla
⅔ cup Hershey's cocoa	
⅓ cup butter or margarine, softened	

Combine confectioners' sugar and cocoa in a bowl. Cream butter or margarine and ½ cup of the cocoa mixture in a large mixer bowl until well blended. Gradually add milk and vanilla. Blend in remaining cocoa mixture, beating to a spreadable consistency.

THE HEILMAN HOUSE
Annville

THE HEILMAN HOUSE On July 6, 1983, Ray and Maggie Coble—he a former ad man and she a former nurse—fulfilled the dreams of many a disciple of Julia Child, Craig Claiborne and Jacques Pepin. They bought an old house, spent two hectic months fixing it up and opened a culinary boutique—a small, select restaurant where just a handful of guests dine luxuriously on the specialties the hosts decide to prepare that day.

The Heilman House is named for the dentist who moved into the 1809 stone house, with its 1885 addition, in 1932. Dining there today is like going to the home of the finest, most caring cook you know and being treated like an honored guest.

You are welcomed by bubbly, smiling Maggie Coble, dressed not like the extraordinary pastry chef she is by day but like the gracious hostess she is at night, in a long gown. She shows you to the Library, where you are offered an apéritif and hors d'oeuvre. Don't overdo it, for you are about to be served a sumptuous six-course feast.

You might be seated in the Columbine Room, where you will dine off specially made rose spatterware decorated with a columbine. Or you may be ushered into the Rose Room, where you will be served on English Spode that has been passed down in Ray's family.

Your first decision will be which of four appetizers to select. Then comes the salad course, always superb at The Heilman House. Except for a Caesar Salad, the Cobles prefer artful and delicious composed salads to the simpler tossed ones.

The soups are peers of the salads. In winter, a lemony Avgolemono or a lusty French Onion Soup is likely to be offered. In summer, it may be Cold Leek Soup or Cold Tomato Soup with Mint.

The choice of entrées normally includes one beef, one seafood, one veal and one "other." When I visited, the "other" was Sweetbreads with Morels. Often it is game. Although I rarely order steak except in a steakhouse, I might make an exception next time I am at The Heilman House, which serves fork-tender Black Angus beef and always creates something interesting with it.

At last, while coffee is poured from an antique urn, you select from four daily desserts. I couldn't resist the dreamy Heilman House Torte: chocolate genoise and almond pastry filled with rum chocolate cream and covered with a chocolate glaze. Maggie Coble has been asked to do a dessert cookbook, so she won't part with any of those recipes. You'll have to visit The Heilman House to get a luscious dessert made by Maggie Coble herself.—c.w.

The Heilman House is located at 115 West Main Street in Annville, 6 miles outside of Hershey. Dinner is served from 6:30 p.m. until 9:00 p.m., Tuesday through Saturday. For reservations (required) call (717) 867-2080.

THE HEILMAN HOUSE'S GRAPEFRUIT SALAD
WITH ROSEMARY CREAM DRESSING

Rosemary Cream Dressing:

1 whole egg
1 egg yolk
½ teaspoon salt
2 teaspoons white
   champagne vinegar
¾ cup good quality olive oil

6 to 8 tablespoons heavy
   cream
1 tablespoon confectioners'
   sugar
juice of ½ lemon
2 teaspoons ground
   rosemary

First make mayonnaise by thoroughly beating egg, egg yolk, salt and champagne vinegar, then adding the olive oil in a thin, steady stream, continuing to beat until mayonnaise is thick. Set aside. Whip cream until soft peaks form, and sweeten with confectioners' sugar. Into the mayonnaise, fold the whipped cream, lemon juice and rosemary. Chill at least one hour.

1 head radicchio, cored,
   washed and leaves
   separated

6 ruby red grapefruit,
   peeled and sectioned
Rosemary Cream Dressing

Just before serving, arrange radicchio leaves, stem ends toward the center, on chilled salad plates. Place grapefruit sections on center and top with chilled Rosemary Cream Dressing. Serves 6.

THE HEILMAN HOUSE'S SALAD CHEVRE

6 ½-inch thick disks of goat cheese (chèvre or Montrachet)
1¼ cup virgin olive oil
2 to 3 tablespoons 25-year-old Spanish sherry wine vinegar
½ cup fresh breadcrumbs (preferably from good French bread)
1 pound fresh spinach, washed and stemmed
2 teaspoons fresh thyme

Marinate the goat cheese in ½ cup olive oil for four hours. Meanwhile, prepare a vinaigrette of the remaining olive oil and the wine vinegar. Preheat oven to 450 degrees. Lightly coat the cheese disks with breadcrumbs. Place on a lightly oiled cookie sheet and bake for 5 minutes (don't overbake). Meanwhile, toss spinach with vinaigrette. Arrange spinach in 6 individual salad bowls or on salad plates. Top each with baked cheese, garnish with thyme and serve immediately. Serves 6.

THE HEILMAN HOUSE'S SHRIMP GRENADA

½ pound large shrimp
½ cup clarified butter
1 to 2 garlic cloves, minced
2 drops Tabasco sauce
½ teaspoon salt (or to taste)
pepper to taste
juice of 1 lime
1 to 2 ounces tequila
chopped fresh parsley

Shell, devein and butterfly shrimp, leaving tails on. Heat butter in a sauté pan and add shrimp. Add garlic and Tabasco, and sauté until the shrimp begin to turn pink, about 2 to 3 minutes. Add salt, pepper, lime juice and tequila. Remove from range and ignite. When the flame dies down, top with parsley and serve immediately. Serves 4.

MARIA'S OLD FORT INN
Lebanon

MARIA'S OLD FORT INN

If central casting were looking for an Italian mama, Maria Mangano, the genial *patronne* of Maria's Old Fort Inn, would be a suitable candidate. A grandmother who favors simple dresses covered by an ample chef's apron, indefatigable Maria is the chief cook and guiding spirit behind this family-style restaurant, where the most popular southern Italian dishes are dispensed in generous portions and at moderate prices.

Maria's husband, Diego, who had a furniture factory in Palermo, Sicily, where Maria ran a grocery store, was the one who urged her to start a restaurant. Maria says he does the simple culinary chores (among which she ranks breadmaking, a task that most of us figure is complicated). Maria prepares everything else—hearty dishes, made from scratch and by feel. I wanted her Gnocchi recipe, but she said that was impossible, since the proportions for this delicious dumpling vary according to temperature and humidity. Maria says you have to feel when the consistency is right.

I did persuade her to tell me the secret of her excellent Minestrone, a vegetable and bean soup so rich that it is almost a meal in itself. She makes it by feel as well, but her estimates of weights and measures of the many ingredients turned out to be an excellent and accurate rendition of the soup I had at the restaurant. Maria's pastas are good, too: spaghetti with a choice of sauces, or such traditional dishes as Lasagna, Ravioli, Baked Ziti and Stuffed Shells, prepared in proper portions of noodles to cheeses to fillings to sauce. The menu also has a selection of seafood and a smaller choice of meat entrées. All the standards are there: Lobster Tail, Shrimp or Seafood Fra Diavolo, Shrimp ala Marinara and Veal Scallopine, with or without Marsala Sauce.

Southern Italian dishes are unusual products to come from a Pennsylvania stone house almost two centuries old. The building, on the outskirts of Lebanon, was erected as an office for the Union Canal, which linked Reading on the Schuylkill River and Middletown on the Susquehanna. The wonderfully proportioned stone structure was, for a time, an apartment building, with a seedy bar called the Old Fort Inn located in an annex. When the Manganos took over the building in the late 1970s, they renovated the first floor of the main house into a casual, comfortable bar and restaurant. But Maria told me that they decided to append her name to that of the previous pub so that locals would know where the place was. Such identification is no longer necessary, for everyone in Lebanon knows where to go when there's a suggestion to have a meal at Maria's.—c.w.

Maria's Old Fort Inn is located at 72 North Maple Street (Route 72) in Lebanon. The restaurant is open Monday through Friday from 11:30 a.m. until 11:00 p.m.; Saturday from 4:00 p.m. until 11:00 p.m.; and Sunday from 2:00 p.m. to 11:00 p.m. Reservations are not customary, but the telephone number is (717) 272-8756.

MARIA'S OLD FORT INN'S STUFFED MUSHROOMS

2 cups plain breadcrumbs
1 teaspoon minced garlic
½ teaspoon black pepper
1 tablespoon chopped parsley
½ teaspoon paprika
2 pounds mushrooms, cleaned and stemmed
¾ cup vegetable oil

Mix breadcrumbs, garlic, pepper, parsley, paprika and oil. Preheat oven to 400 degrees. Mound breadcrumb mixture in each mushroom. Place on a lightly oiled cookie sheet and bake for 20 minutes. Serves 10 to 12 as an appetizer.

MARIA'S OLD FORT INN'S LASAGNA

2 tablespoons oil
1 small onion, chopped
3 pounds ground beef
1½ pounds lasagna noodles
1 pound Ricotta cheese
½ pound Mozzarella cheese, cubed
¼ pound Parmesan cheese, grated
3 cups homemade tomato sauce

In a large saucepan, heat oil and sauté onion until wilted. Add meat, stirring frequently to break apart chunks, until browned. Meanwhile, cook lasagna noodles in boiling water according to package directions. Drain. Mix the three cheeses together. Remove browned meat with a slotted spoon and mix into cheeses. Preheat oven to 350 degrees. Place a small amount of sauce into the bottom of a large, ungreased baking pan. Add a layer of noodles, top with one-half of the meat and cheese mixture and one-half of the remaining sauce. Repeat layers. Bake for about 30 minutes, until bubbling hot. Let stand 10 minutes before serving. Serves 10 to 12.

MARIA'S OLD FORT INN'S MINESTRONE

dried lentils, peas, white and red beans, chickpeas and barley according to taste, totaling 1 pound
1 onion, chopped
2 potatoes, peeled and diced
4 stalks celery, diced
2 10-ounce packages frozen mixed vegetables
1 cup tomato sauce, home-made or canned
¼ pound small tubular macaroni
2 garlic cloves, chopped
salt and pepper to taste
2 to 4 tablespoons oil

Bring two quarts of water to a boil. Add beans, onion, potatoes and celery. Cover and simmer over a very low flame, approximately 2½ hours. More water may be added if necessary. Add frozen mixed vegetables and tomato sauce and cook for 5 minutes. Add macaroni and garlic and cook for 5 to 7 minutes, until macaroni is tender, taking care that water does not boil away. Add salt, pepper and oil. Serves 8 to 10.

THE GEORGE WASHINGTON TAVERN
Lebanon

THE GEORGE WASHINGTON TAVERN

This fine old stone building in the heart of Lebanon has been offering hospitality to travelers and diners since 1760, when it was built as The Farmer's Hotel. George Washington—accompanied by Daniel Rittenhouse, Robert Morris, Dr. William Smith and Tench Francis—stayed there when they came to inspect the new Union Canal in 1792.

Current owner Abe Harounzadeh, who worked his way through college in the late 1960s and early 1970s as a restaurant manager in Boston, is Iranian-born. Although the restaurant specializes in Italian and French dishes, Harounzadeh occasionally sneaks in a bit of a Middle Eastern touch to remind him of home, like the Pheasant with Walnut Sauce and other exotic fare that he whips up for special groups.

I was intrigued by the restaurant's look. There is the low ceiling one would expect in an eighteenth-century inn, but there are terrazzo floors that astonish anyone expecting random-length pine. When I learned that the dining room was added in the 1930s, the stone floor was no longer such a surprise—nor were the comfortable banquettes that reminded me of eating places in old Hollywood movies.

I loved the bar, which is in the oldest part of the building. The fireplace, as large as a walk-in closet, is surrounded by comfortable sofas to sink into. In the early 1900s, a Hershey artist whose name is lost to memory painted a frieze depicting events in George Washington's life around the walls of this cozy room. A mural showing how the inn looked in 1760 graces the dining room, which also is decorated with antique farm implements.

Dinner at The George Washington Tavern can be a lovely production. Many dishes are prepared at the table. Four veal entrées are finished in a copper pan tableside, each one splashed with a different wine. The waiter expertly debones the English Dover Sole or whips up a Caesar Salad at the table, and if you order Cherries Jubilee, Peach Flambé, Bananas Foster, Crêpes Suzette or Strawberries Flambé (a summer specialty), he will flame those for you, too.

114

While The George Washington Tavern serves sinfully rich pasta, it is also a place where calorie counters have a fine choice. A Fresh Jumbo Shrimp Cocktail or Fresh Florida Fruit Cup makes a nonfattening appetizer, and the simply sautéed Veal Piccante is even described on the menu as a dieter's delight.—c.w.

The George Washington Tavern is located on the corner of Tenth and Cumberland streets in Lebanon. Dinner is served from 5:00 p.m. until 9:30 p.m., Sunday through Tuesday, and from 5:00 p.m. until 10:00 p.m., Friday and Saturday. For reservations (requested) call (717) 274-1233.

THE GEORGE WASHINGTON TAVERN'S
FETTUCINI ROYAL

¼ pound fettucini, cooked
½ cup cream cheese, melted
4 tablespoons Rhine wine
½ cup backfin crabmeat
1 tablespoon chopped
  parsley

2 tablespoons freshly grated
  Parmesan cheese
salt and pepper to taste

Drain the cooked fettucini in a colander. In a saucepan over low heat, combine the melted cream cheese, wine and crabmeat and heat through. Add the fettucini and parsley, and toss. Place on individual plates or a small serving platter. Top with Parmesan cheese, a sprinkling of salt and a grating of pepper. Serves 2.

THE GEORGE WASHINGTON TAVERN'S
VEAL DIJONNAISE

4 to 5 tablespoons flour
4 6-ounce medallions of
  veal
3 tablespoons sweet butter
2 tablespoons Dijon
  mustard

½ cup chopped mushrooms
⅓ cup Chablis wine
½ cup cream cheese, melted
salt and pepper to taste

115

Lightly flour the veal medallions. In a medium skillet, melt butter and add veal. Sauté 2 to 3 minutes on each side. Meanwhile, mix remaining ingredients and pour over veal. Cook uncovered over medium heat for five minutes. Serves 4.

THE GEORGE WASHINGTON TAVERN'S
STRAWBERRIES FLAMBE

12 large strawberries, sliced
⅓ cup granulated sugar

4 ounces strawberry-
flavored brandy
vanilla ice cream

Place strawberries in a shallow copper pan over a medium flame. Add sugar and 2 ounces brandy. Stir quickly and cook until liquid becomes syrupy. Add remaining brandy and ignite as you tilt the pan. Turn off the heat and continue stirring until the flame dies down. Serve over vanilla ice cream. Serves 2.

THE OLDE DANISH INN
Myerstown

**THE OLDE
DANISH INN**

The inn in the micro-hamlet of Myerstown has had a checkered history indeed. It was built in 1890 as Weaver's Hotel, a coach stop between Reading and Harrisburg. That, of course, wasn't terribly long before horsedrawn coaches went out of favor.

The building passed through several hands during the decades that followed—which included two world wars and the Depression—and during that time was called the Millardsville Hotel. By the late 1960s, it was a beer joint that drew all the rogues from miles around. Many people in Lebanon County remember being served their first drink there, and stories are still told of wild beer bashes downstairs and terrific poker games upstairs.

In 1976, the inn was purchased by Kaj Skov, an energetic Dane who had come to this country in 1968 to work as a chef at a Philadelphia country club. Skov eventually bought a restaurant in nearby Elizabethtown, and when the old inn became available, he bought it, too.

While he was cleaning out the basement, he found four old wooden letters among the rubble. When the proper anagram was composed, the letters spelled SKOL, the Scandinavian toast. "Not that I'm superstitious," Skov now says, "but poor as I was, I felt there was a reason they were here." He turned the basement into a lounge and hung the letters over the bar. The omen was a good one, though Skov didn't realize it immediately; the day he opened he had but one customer. But it didn't take long for the word to get out. The restaurant became so busy that he sold the Elizabethtown place.

The Olde Danish Inn at lunch is clublike, with the same customers from nearby businesses meeting and eating every day. I was there for dinner, happily nibbling on Fried Troutlings while perusing the menu filled with Danish and other Continental dishes. The Troutlings, which don't appear on the menu, are two-inch fishlets from a hatchery down the road that are dipped in flour and cracker meal, deep-fried till crispy and served with a tomato dipping sauce.

It isn't every day you find a fine Scandinavian restaurant in the rural countryside, so I started with a delicious Marinated Herring in Sour Cream Sauce. Kaj Skov insisted that I try the Frikkadeller, a pair of Danish meat patties served with traditional side dishes of red cabbage and cucumber salad. The Olde Danish Inn also offers some unusual casseroles, such as the Casserole Elsinor with veal, shrimp and vegetables and the Hans Christian Andersen Casserole with chicken, pork and mushrooms. My companion opted for a New York Strip Béarnaise, and found it first-rate. Desserts run to pies, mousses and ice cream, plus Kransekage, which are Danish petits fours.—c.w.

The Olde Danish Inn is located at 890 Tulpehocken Road two miles east of Myerstown. Lunch is served from 11:30 a.m. until 2:00 p.m., Monday through Friday. Dinner is served from 5:00 p.m. until 10:00 p.m., Tuesday through Saturday. For reservations (required) call (717) 866-7311.

THE OLDE DANISH INN'S FRIKKADELLER

½ pound ground lean pork
½ pound ground veal
2 eggs, lightly beaten
3 tablespoons flour
¼ to ½ cup milk

1 medium onion, chopped
salt and pepper to taste
2 to 3 tablespoons
  margarine
2 cups brown gravy

Combine pork and veal; set aside. Mix eggs, flour and milk. (If your pork is very lean, you may use the entire ½ cup of milk; if it is somewhat fatty, use less.) Work the egg mixture and the onion into the pork-veal mixture, together with salt and pepper. Refrigerate for 15 to 20 minutes so that the mixture becomes firm enough to shape. (If it becomes too firm, add a little water.) Shape into meatballs about the size of limes and flatten slightly. Heat margarine in a skillet and fry the patties until well done on each side. Add gravy to the skillet and heat. Serves 6 to 8.

119

THE OLDE DANISH INN'S SPINACH SALAD
WITH DILL DRESSING

Dill Dressing:

2 cups sour cream

1 bunch fresh dill, stemmed and finely chopped

1 small onion, finely chopped

juice of ½ lemon

salt and pepper to taste

Mix all ingredients. Chill.

1 pound fresh spinach, washed thoroughly, stemmed and dried

½ pound fresh mushrooms, sliced

1 cup croutons

Toss spinach and mushrooms with Dill Dressing, top with croutons and serve immediately. Serves 12.

THE OLDE DANISH INN'S
HANS CHRISTIAN ANDERSEN CASSEROLE

4 tablespoons oil or margarine

1 pound chicken breast, skinned, boned and cubed

1 pound pork tenderloin, cubed

salt and pepper to taste

1 medium onion, chopped

½ pound fresh mushrooms, sliced

1 tablespoon brandy

1 cup Burgundy

2 cups brown gravy

Heat oil or margarine in a skillet. Add chicken and pork, seasoned with salt and pepper, and sauté over medium-high heat, stirring frequently, until golden. Add onion and sauté until onion is tender. Stir in mushrooms. Stir in brandy and Burgundy. Simmer until liquid is reduced by one-half. Stir in gravy. Simmer for several minutes until heated through. Serves 6.

STOKESAY CASTLE
Reading

STOKESAY CASTLE   Sitting majestically atop a hill, Stokesay Castle seems the perfect setting for a romance novel—especially when you discover its romantic origins. George Hiester and his bride fell in love with the original Stokesay Castle in Shropshire, England, while they were on their honeymoon. After returning to the United States in 1931, Hiester had an exact replica of the 1240 castle built.

The magnificence of this structure rising out of the snow made me wonder where you find men who are willing to throw together a little castle for you. Apparently no expense was spared, as the stone is authentically sculpted.

My friend Karen Afflerbach and I began our repast in the triple-tier vaulted Great Hall beside a warm fire. We ordered a Chablis and were invited to see where wine is stored. Appropriately, it was protected by bars in the Keep Tavern Rathskeller.

Continuing our tour, we made the long climb to the tower. Our efforts were rewarded with a thirty-mile view that was absolutely breathtaking.

At our table, between sips of wine and bites of the Stokesay Green Salade with Hot Bacon Dressing, I spoke to manager Scott Quade. Right after Stokesay's Famous Beef Stroganoff arrived, I heard about their female spirit. As I savored the hearty yet gently spiced entrée, I learned that the spirit loves to play little pranks at closing time. Once, the center rack holding wine glasses crashed to the floor, an incident that can't be explained, since the outer supporting racks held firm. The ghost has never materialized when guests are present, but she keeps the staff on its toes.

Although Stokesay Castle's atmosphere can carry you right back to an Olde English winter, I look forward to returning in the summer for outdoor dining with a mountain view—and another nibble of their superb Carrot Cake.

Stokesay Castle is located on Hill Road and Spook Lane in Reading. Lunch is served from 11:30 a.m. until 3:30 p.m., Monday through Saturday. Dinner is served from 4:00 p.m.

until 9:30 p.m., Monday through Friday, and from 4:00 p.m. until 10:00 p.m. on Saturday. Sunday dinner is served from noon until 8:00 p.m. For reservations (preferred) call (215) 375-4588.

STOKESAY CASTLE'S FAMOUS BEEF STROGANOFF

1½ pounds tenderloin strips
4 tablespoons butter
1 cup fresh mushrooms, sliced
1 cup Brown Sauce (recipe below)

¾ cup sour cream
wild rice (cook according to package diections)

Sauté tenderloin strips in butter. Add mushrooms and sauté until tender. Drain butter and add Brown Sauce, stirring until well blended. Add sour cream and stir until heated through. Serve over cooked wild rice. Serves 6.

STOKESAY CASTLE'S BROWN SAUCE

5 tablespoons butter
3 tablespoons oil
3 carrots, sliced
2 medium onions, sliced
1 celery rib, sliced
1 stick butter
½ cup flour
8 cups beef stock or beef broth (commercial or homemade)

2 tablespoons tomato paste
1 garlic clove, chopped
9 sprigs parsley
2 teaspoons thyme
1 bay leaf
1 pound chicken, beef or ham bones
¼ cup sherry
salt and pepper to taste

Heat butter and oil together in a large soup pot. Brown carrots, onions and celery in butter-oil mixture; remove vegetables and reserve. In the same pot, melt the remaining stick of butter over low heat. Add flour and stir to make a roux. Add beef stock a little at a time. Increase heat and stir until boiling. Add reserved vegetables to soup pot with tomato paste, garlic, parsley, thyme, bay leaf and bones. Reduce heat and simmer. Skim scum from the top and cook until volume is reduced and

123

sauce is thick (at least 3 hours). Stir periodically to prevent sticking. Before using add sherry and salt and pepper. Yields approximately 1 quart.

NOTE: Can be frozen and used to cook with veal and other cuts of meat.

STOKESAY CASTLE'S VEAL PICANTE

1 pound thin veal cutlet
½ cup flour
2 tablespoons butter
pinch of garlic powder

1 cup fresh mushrooms, sliced
¾ cup white wine
fresh parsley

Pound veal with a meat mallet until thin and pliable. Cut into four equal pieces. Dust veal with flour. Melt butter in a skillet and sauté veal. Add garlic powder, mushrooms and white wine. Stir over high heat until sauce thickens slightly. Remove veal and garnish with parsley. Serves 4.

WIDOW FINNEY'S
Reading

WIDOW FINNEY'S

Part of the joy of writing this sort of book is discovering history's unrecorded heroines and heroes. Just such a discovery materialized at Widow Finney's. The story goes that after Sarah Finney's husband, Joseph, and her sons died in 1734, the widow had a tough time holding her claim to the property that she and her family had cleared and tilled. The problem occurred when William Penn's sons, realizing that the land had become a choice property, tried to retrieve it. To the surprise of the Penns, the spunky widow got a court order protecting her right to the land.

After the widow took account of her assets, she decided that her survival depended on opening her home to travelers. Word of this courageous lady's hospitality spread, making her Reading's first hostess, and in time her homestead became known as Widow Finney's place.

Over two hundred years later, Susan Brubaker and Arlene Unger walked past the picturesque but vacant and rundown Log House, John Hiester House and the West Reading Market Annex, all located one block away from the Widow's original home. Brubaker's and Unger's sense of history was so stirred that they purchased the Log House and undertook its restoration. In the restored building they housed a restaurant, which they named in honor of the widow who had lived and worked nearby.

Like me, Brubaker and Unger are interested in the contributions that so many women—not just the famous ones—have made to America. Not the least of women's achievements has been the development of American cookery. At Widow Finney's, as in many restaurants I've visited, I found such contributions at last receiving their just recognition.

Sitting beside a warm fireplace in the Great Room, I was easily persuaded to try a Seyval Blanc from Bucks County Vineyards. As I sipped, I admired the walls of log and stone, chinked with river clay and straw. The adjoining dining room is nostalgically simple, with bouquets of herbs hung from open hand-hewn beams. Because Brubaker and Unger wanted their guests to dine in an atmosphere completely representative of colonial life, the only lighting is by candle. The colonial décor complements the recipes, which the two women developed from their research on recipes dating as far back as the seventeenth century.

Munching on their freshly baked Poppy Seed Bread and a fabulous yeast bread shaped in knots, I feared that I would stuff myself before my entrée arrived. But I found room for Oysters Jenny Lind, a combination of oysters and ham in a cream sauce served over puff pastry. The Carrots Dijon accompanying this entrée were so fresh and unusually seasoned that I asked for the recipe on the spot.

The Ecclefechan, or Scottish Fruit Tart, turned out to be much tastier than the Christmas fruitcakes belonging to the same family. This rich treat was the perfect finale to an evening that was as close as you can come to dining in our colonial past.

Widow Finney's is located at Fourth and Cherry streets in Reading. Lunch is served from 11:00 a.m. until 2:00 p.m., Monday through Saturday. Dinner is served from 5:30 p.m. until 8:00 p.m., Wednesday through Saturday. For reservations (suggested) call (215) 378-1776.

WIDOW FINNEY'S ECCLEFECHAN
(Scottish Fruit Tart)

Crust:

3 cups all-purpose flour	6 tablespoons sugar
7½ ounces cold butter, cubed	3 egg yolks

Combine all ingredients in the bowl of an electric mixer or food processor (if using a food processor, use knife attachment and an on-off technique). Blend until ball forms. Divide dough in half and refrigerate for a half hour. Roll each ball into a round to fit two 9-inch tart pans. Press dough evenly into place, coming about 1 inch up the side of pan. (These tarts are best made in pans with removable bottoms.)

127

Filling:

6 ounces dried apricots	3 eggs
4 ounces raisins	6 ounces butter, melted
2 ounces dried, pitted prunes	3 tablespoons red wine vinegar
3 ounces walnuts	

Chop dried fruits and nuts by hand until very small (do not use food processor). Combine eggs, butter and wine vinegar until well mixed. Add fruits and nuts to mixture and stir by hand until thoroughly combined. Divide evenly between the two tart shells and bake at 375 degrees for 30 to 35 minutes. Serve warm or at room temperature. Yields two 9-inch tarts.

NOTE: These tarts freeze well.

WIDOW FINNEY'S CARROTS DIJON

1 tablespoon butter	dash of salt
1 tablespoon honey	1 pound can baby carrots
2 teaspoons Dijon mustard	

In a medium saucepan over low heat, melt butter and add honey; stir until smooth. Add mustard and salt and stir until combined. Add baby carrots and heat for 3 to 4 minutes. Serves 4.

BLAIR CREEK INN
Mertztown

BLAIR CREEK INN

Amid farmyards and corn- fields is the welcoming yellow canopy of the Blair Creek Inn. Housed in a sturdy former farmhouse, the restaurant has been renovated into a historically respectful but far more elegant structure than it originally was.

The innkeeper, Blair Henry, studied cooking on the GI Bill in France, Germany and Switzerland. In 1977, he created what has turned into one of Pennsylvania's loveliest restaurants. Blair confesses to being a frustrated florist in addition to a restaurateur. During the warm months, he's up at dawn, cutting and arranging garden-fresh flowers for all the tables and even the restrooms, and he urges guests to stroll around the inn's six exquisite acres before or after dining.

Four lovely dining rooms are filled with antiques Blair has brought back from his world travels. I especially loved the main dining room, called the Vienna Room after the brass candle chandelier that belonged to the Austrian Imperial household. The room is papered in a warm rose-beige moire, and on one wall, small glass cases display thirteen original Boehm birds, the first flock that brought this potter international fame.

The inn was built in 1847 as a Quaker meeting house, but with the area's prevailing Moravian, Amish and Mennonite influences, the Quakers never gained a foothold here. In 1849, the building was doubled in size and the property became a farm. By the 1970s, it was a shabby tavern serving two beers for fifteen cents and hoagies for twenty-nine.

Happily, those days belong to history. The Blair Creek Inn's dinners are now carefully prepared, exquisitely garnished and formally served. I visited in summer, when the Cold Gazpacho arrived tantalizingly chilled. A separate compartmentalized Spanish platter contains a selection of traditional condiments. In winter, the Cuban Black Bean Soup is similarly served. Pheasant en Croute, Sweetbreads Under Glass and Veal Habsburg are elegant names for elegant entrées.

The Blair Creek Inn's brunch features fine renditions of Portuguese Eggs, Quiche Lorraine or Chicken Salad Empress, which can launch anyone's week in a grand fashion.—C.W.

The Blair Creek Inn is located on Main Street in Mertztown. Dinner is served from 5:30 p.m. until 9:30 p.m., Tuesday through Saturday. Sunday brunch is served from 10:30 a.m. until 1:30 p.m. For reservations (required) call (215) 682-6700 or (215) 682-4101.

BLAIR CREEK INN'S CUBAN BLACK BEAN SOUP

1 pound black beans
2 quarts water
2 tablespoons salt
2 tablespoons vegetable oil
3 garlic cloves, minced
1 cup chopped onions

¾ cup chopped green bell peppers
1½ teaspoons cumin
1½ teaspoons oregano
2 tablespoons cider vinegar

Garnish:
2 to 3 cups cooked rice
½ cup diced onions

2 to 3 hard-boiled eggs, chopped fine

Soak beans in 1 quart of water overnight; then add another quart of water and the salt. Cover beans and bring to a boil. Lower heat to simmer and cook until beans are soft. In a skillet heat the oil and sauté garlic, onions and peppers until tender. Add spices and vinegar, mixing well, and add to the beans. Cook slowly, uncovered, for at least 1 hour. Garnish with cold rice, diced onions and chopped eggs. Serves 10 to 12.

BLAIR CREEK INN'S FRANGELICO CHEESECAKE

1 pound cream cheese, softened
½ cup sugar
1 tablespoon flour
2 large eggs
2 tablespoons Frangelico liqueur

⅔ cup hazelnuts, toasted and skinned
1 graham cracker crust (see index) baked in a 7- or 9-inch springform pan

Preheat oven to 350 degrees. In a large bowl, cream together cream cheese, sugar and flour. Beat in eggs, one at a time, beating well after each addition, and continue beating until mixture is smooth. Stir in Frangelico and one-half of the hazelnuts. Pour the filling into the crust and bake in the middle of the oven until filling is set, 30 to 35 minutes. Place the cheesecake on a rack to cool. Meanwhile, finely chop remaining hazelnuts and sprinkle on cake. Chill for 2 hours. Yields one cheesecake.

BLAIR CREEK INN'S LIVER DUMPLING SOUP

4 stale Kaiser rolls
½ cup lukewarm milk
9 ounces beef liver, trimmed
2 tablespoons sweet butter
1 medium onion, finely chopped
1 bunch parsley, finely chopped

2 eggs, lightly beaten
marjoram, salt, pepper and chopped chives, to taste
1 quart beef stock (commercial or homemade)
chopped chives for garnish

Cut rolls into thin slices and place in a deep bowl. Add milk and stir to soak. Meanwhile, grind liver in a food mill and set aside. Melt butter in a skillet and sauté onion and parsley until wilted. Mix all ingredients but the stock and the garnish with the soaked rolls and form into four large dumplings. Heat the stock until it begins to boil. Carefully drop the dumplings into the stock and simmer for 20 minutes. Place one dumpling in each of four soup dishes, top with stock and sprinkle with chives. Serves 4.

YE OLDE LIMEPORT HOTEL
Limeport

YE OLDE LIMEPORT HOTEL

One March night, Kay and Richard McGowen were awakened by the distinct cry of a child's voice calling "Mom, Mom," under the window of their apartment in Ye Olde Limeport Hotel. Kay went downstairs to investigate, but no one was there. Several similar incidents occurred, but the McGowens thought little of them until an elderly lady who grew up in the area said she never again wanted to be seated in the inn's Red Room. "Too many spirits," she announced. The McGowens weren't totally surprised, for they knew that mass was said and wakes were held in that room before there was a Catholic Church in the vicinity.

Months later, the McGowens learned from another senior citizen the possible source of the ghost they had heard calling. It seems that Wilson Henry, who had owned the hotel in the early years of the twentieth century, and his twelve-year-old son had died (during an influenza epidemic) in a bedchamber just above the Red Room. It was then that the McGowens realized why their otherwise courageous Great Dane, Maisey, steadfastly refused to enter that bedroom.

The restaurant is old enough to have had many ghosts. It was built in 1842 by Joseph Wittman, a prosperous local storekeeper, as a stagecoach stop. Now it is a rollicking Irish bar and pleasant restaurant. Dick McGowen—probably decked out in a kelly green shirt and definitely with handlebar mustache nicely waxed—often presides at the bar. Perch on a stool, admire the Irish artifacts and order a Guinness, or perhaps one of Dick's own inventions. He has even concocted a drink that resembles a Reese's Peanut Butter Cup.

Alcohol is also a key ingredient in many of the specialties served at Ye Olde Limeport Inn. It's amazing what a dose of Irish whiskey will do for chicken or how fruit brandy will enhance a mousse.

Both cozy dining rooms are paneled in rough pine, decked out with arrangements of dried flowers, and have tables covered with flower-print cloths. The effect is so cheerful that it's no wonder the ghost waits until lights out before asking to enter.—C.W.

134

Ye Olde Limeport Hotel is located on Limeport Pike in Limeport. Lunch is served from 11:00 a.m. until 5:00 p.m., Tuesday through Friday. Dinner is served from 5:00 p.m. until 9:00 p.m., Tuesday through Thursday; from 5:00 p.m. until 11:00 p.m., Friday and Saturday; and from 1:00 p.m. until 8:00 p.m. on Sunday during the winter, and until 9:00 during the summer. For reservations (requested) call (215) 967-1810.

YE OLDE LIMEPORT HOTEL'S PEANUT BUTTER CUP

⅔ cup ice cubes
1 heaping tablespoon smooth peanut butter
1 ounce vodka
2 ounces creme de cacao

half and half
whipped cream
unsalted roast peanuts, chopped

Put ice cubes, peanut butter, vodka and creme de cacao into the container of a blender. Pour in half and half to cover the ice cubes. Blend at high speed until mixture is smooth. Pour into a glass, top with whipped cream and sprinkle with chopped peanuts. Serves 1.

YE OLDE LIMEPORT HOTEL'S GALWAY CHICKEN

2 boneless chicken breasts, about 7 ounces each
2 cups unseasoned bread-crumbs
⅓ cup Irish whiskey
¼ teaspoon celery seed
½ teaspoon dried parsley

¼ teaspoon thyme
chicken stock or water (optional)
4 strips bacon
½ cup Irish whiskey
½ cup chicken stock

Preheat oven to 375 degrees. Pound chicken breasts lightly to flatten. Mix breadcrumbs, whiskey, seasonings and, if you like a moist stuffing, a small amount of water or stock. Place crumb mixture on chicken breasts, roll and fasten with wooden toothpicks. Place in a baking pan and top with bacon. Bake 30 minutes. Meanwhile, combine whiskey and ½ cup chicken stock in a small saucepan and bring to a boil. Lower heat and reduce by half. Remove chicken to a serving platter, pull out toothpicks and pour whiskey sauce over chicken. Serves 2.

YE OLDE LIMEPORT HOTEL'S GAELIC STEAK

2 New York strip steaks,   1 cup Irish whiskey
  about 10 ounces each   ½ cup heavy cream
½ cup chopped onion
½ cup sliced fresh
  mushrooms

Heat a large, heavy iron skillet until very hot. Sear steak on both sides. Lower heat and cook steak to desired doneness, adding onion and mushrooms partway through the cooking process. Remove pan from heat, pour whiskey over steaks, and flame. When flame has died down, remove the steaks to a warm platter. Lower heat and return skillet to range. Stir in cream, heat briefly and pour over steaks. Serves 2.

YE OLDE LIMEPORT HOTEL'S PEACH MOUSSE

2 ripe peaches   ½ cup sugar
4 eggs, separated   whipped cream
½ teaspoon vanilla extract
¼ cup peach brandy
  (schnapps)

Wash peaches (do not peel) and chop fine. Combine egg yolks, peaches and vanilla. In a saucepan over low heat, cook peach mixture for 20 minutes, stirring frequently. Add peach brandy. Set aside to cool. Beat egg whites until stiff, adding sugar during beating. Fold peach mixture into egg whites. Chill. Serve with whipped cream. Serves 4.

KING GEORGE INN
Allentown

KING GEORGE INN Owner Cliff McDermott is fond of describing the King George Inn as an Irish bar with an English name. This merry establishment at a crossroads that once bore the name Dorneyville is also a local favorite for light lunches and hearty dinners drawn from many popular cuisines. The dinner menu features French-style Chicken Dijonnaise, Italian Veal Picatta and Parmigiana, and made-in-the-U.S.A. Manhattan Clam Chowder and New York Strip Steak, all served in a friendly atmosphere.

When I sat at a table on the flower-bedecked front porch and watched the endless stream of traffic along Hamilton and Cedar Crest boulevards, it was hard to imagine Dorneyville as a sleepy backwater. But in 1756, when Dorney's Tavern was constructed as a stagecoach stop, Dorneyville was a true frontier hamlet.

The settlement's most trying time was an ugly spell during the French and Indian wars, when a band of Indians snatched and murdered several babies and threw them into Dorneyville wells. In 1937, a sixty-three-year-old inn employee inadvertently locked herself into the dark cellar near the well. While waiting to be rescued, she heard so terrifying a baby's cry that she had to be hospitalized for several days.

The well enclosure is now the wine cellar, and the basement itself is a cozy paneled lounge called the Prince of Wales Tavern (photographs of the Royal Wedding line the wall). Sounds of revelry rather than mayhem are now heard in these quarters.

On the main floor, two pleasant dining rooms flank the busiest of the King George Inn's three bars. This bar is decorated with sports memorabilia, including photos of Cliff and Nancy McDermott with various star athletes. For dining, I like the Hearth Room, with its thick exposed stone walls and narrow, perfectly proportioned wooden mantelpiece.

In many other restaurants, two levels for drinking and eating would suffice, but the jovial crowds at the King George Inn often require three. Therefore, the second floor of the old inn has been made into a low-ceilinged, English-style dining

138

room with a large glassed-in extension built over the original porch roof.

The King George Inn is a congenial spot to meet old friends or make new ones—and to share a good meal, good conversation and an overall terrific time.—c.w.

The King George Inn is located at Hamilton and Cedar Crest boulevards in Allentown. Lunch is served from 11:00 a.m. until 4:00 p.m., Monday through Friday. Dinner is served from 4:00 p.m. until 10:00 p.m., Monday through Thursday; from 4:00 p.m. until midnight, Friday and Saturday; and from 4:00 p.m. until 9:00 p.m. on Sunday. For reservations (recommended) call (215) 435-1723.

KING GEORGE INN'S CAESAR SALAD

1 large head romaine lettuce	½ teaspoon freshly ground black pepper
half of a 2-ounce can anchovies	1 egg, beaten
1 teaspoon finely chopped garlic	½ cup lemon juice
	¼ cup good-quality olive oil
½ teaspoon Worcestershire sauce	½ cup freshly grated Parmesan cheese
½ teaspoon dry mustard	¼ cup croutons (recipe below)

Separate lettuce leaves, wash well and tear green portion into bite-sized pieces, discarding stalks. Place anchovies in a large wooden salad bowl and crush with the back of a spoon. Add garlic, Worcestershire sauce, mustard, pepper, egg, lemon juice and olive oil. Whip ingredients until well blended and slightly frothy. Add lettuce. Toss. Top with cheese and croutons. Serve on cold glass plates. Serves 2.

Croutons:

1 or 2 slices French bread, slightly stale	1 tablespoon oil
	1 garlic clove

Cut bread into ½-inch cubes. Heat oil in small skillet until hot but not smoking. Meanwhile, peel garlic and halve it lengthwise. Sauté garlic, stirring, until it begins to brown. Remove garlic and stir in bread cubes. Sauté, stirring, until croutons are lightly browned on all sides.

KING GEORGE INN'S STEAK ALA PIZZIOLA

2 9- to 10-ounce New York
  strip steaks
1 cup Chianti or other dry
  Italian wine
¼ teaspoon fresh basil (or
  pinch dried)
¼ teaspoon fresh tarragon
  (or pinch dried)

salt
½ cup marinara sauce
  (homemade or canned)
4 to 6 large mushrooms,
  thinly sliced
4 large, thin slices
  Mozzarella cheese

Carefully trim all fat and gristle from meat. Mix wine and herbs and marinate meat 7 to 10 minutes. Meanwhile, heat a large, heavy iron skillet until extremely hot. Remove meat from marinade and pat dry. Sprinkle a layer of salt over the bottom of the skillet, add meat and sear. When ready to turn over, resalt skillet. Cook meat to desired doneness. Place steaks on an ovenproof platter. Top each with half the marinara sauce, mushrooms and two slices of Mozzarella. Bake in a 350-degree oven until cheese melts. Serves 2.

NOTE: The steaks may be broiled very close to a very hot flame; not all home ranges have sufficient high-temperature broiling capabilities.

MAIN STREET DEPOT
Bethlehem

MAIN STREET DEPOT When Bethlehem was a busy stop on the thriving Jersey Central rail line, its small brick station, built in 1874, was purely utilitarian. No one paid much attention to its handsome proportions, to its steep mansard roof tiled in hexagonal slate or even to the view across the railroad tracks to the Lehigh Canal.

As railroads gave way to other forms of travel, the lovely little station fell into disuse, and in 1962, the last passenger train left Bethlehem. In just a few years, the station had become such an eyesore that the local Jaycees took it upon themselves to clean up the exterior. But it was not until 1977, when Ralph Mittl of nearby Allentown took the building over and converted it into a restaurant, that its restoration was completed.

Today, the lounge, where the waiting room and stationmaster's office once were, is a medley of old and new. Original tongue-and-groove wainscoting painted apple green, period wallpaper, green plants and rotating fans suspended from the lofty ceiling, and railroad memorabilia make a cozy atmosphere from a space once purely functional.

Downstairs, in a maze of former storage rooms, coal cellars and furnace rooms, is the cozy dining area. Beamed ceilings, leaded-glass lamps over each table and dark walls of old stone create an intimate ambience.

Sandwiches, omelettes and burgers highlight the casual lunch menu, while a more ambitious selection of mainly seafood and meat specialties—many with a Continental accent—is featured at dinner. I visited at midday, so I didn't have a chance to sample the Veal Alaska à la Ralph, but since I assume that the chef always names one of his or her proudest creations after the boss, I suspect that this medley of sliced veal, crabmeat and cheddar cheese sauce is one of the house specialties.

The Main Street Depot also offers less caloric dishes for dieters. Clams or Oysters on the Half-Shell, a Broiled Seafood Combination or the Soup and Salad Bar selection would be appropriate.

142

What is always appropriate is a stop at the Main Street Depot—to drink, to eat or simply to honor its renewal. Bethlehem now has an admirable ongoing program of restoration in its historic central business district. And this pleasant restaurant at the foot of Main Street was one of the first structures to be reclaimed.—c.w.

Main Street Depot is located at Main and Lehigh streets in Bethlehem. Lunch is served from 11:30 a.m. until 2:30 p.m., Monday through Friday. Dinner is served from 4:30 p.m. until 10:00 p.m., Monday through Saturday. For reservations (requested) call (215) 868-7123.

MAIN STREET DEPOT'S CHICKEN GUMBO SOUP

½ pound carrots, scraped
½ pound celery
½ pound onions
¼ pound green pepper, seeded
½ pound fresh mushrooms
½ pound okra

4 quarts chicken stock (canned or homemade)
1 8-ounce can of diced tomato or tomato pieces
¼ pound rice
seasoned salt to taste
white pepper to taste

Cut fresh vegetables into desired shapes (small cubes, slices, bias-cut slices, etc.). Meanwhile, bring stock to a boil in a large pot. Add all fresh vegetables, tomatoes and rice. Allow to come almost to a boil, turn down to a slow simmer and cook, covered, until all vegetables are tender (about 1 hour). Season to taste. Serves 12.

MAIN STREET DEPOT'S SEAFOOD FRITTATA

2 asparagus spears
2 tablespoons sweet butter
3 eggs, well beaten

¼ cup crabmeat
½ medium tomato, chopped

Cook asparagus in boiling water until tender but still crisp. Cut into 4 pieces. Melt butter in medium omelette pan or skillet. Pour in eggs, tilting pan to spread evenly. Top with asparagus, crabmeat and tomato. Do not roll or fold. When egg has set, but before it cooks dry, place pan briefly under broiler to heat toppings. Serve immediately. Serves 1.

MAIN STREET DEPOT'S STEAK DEPOT

¾ pound tenderloin tips	pinch of oregano
½ cup soy sauce	½ cup flour
pinch of ground pepper	oil for frying
pinch of granulated garlic	Onion Straws (recipe below)

Cut meat into 1-inch cubes. Mix soy sauce and seasonings and pour over meat. Marinate for 1 hour. Remove meat from marinade, pat dry and dredge in flour, shaking off excess. Pour oil in a wok or heavy saucepan to a depth sufficient to cover meat. Heat oil to 350 degrees. Drop meat into hot oil and fry until crispy. Remove meat with a slotted spoon, reserving oil for recipe below, and serve with Onion Straws. Serves 2.

Onion Straws:

1 onion, sliced very thin	salt and pepper to taste
flour	oil from frying meat

Dip onion slices into flour seasoned with salt and pepper. Shake off excess. Fry quickly in hot oil in which the meat has been cooked. Remove with a slotted spoon and serve alongside steak.

SUN INN
Bethlehem

SUN INN

In 1787, the Marquis de Chastellux, touring the infant United States with forty other members of the French Academy, raved about what he ate at the Sun Inn: "Venison, moor-game, the most delicious red- and yellow-bellied trout, the highest-flavored wild strawberries, the most luxuriant vegetables." When he penned those words, the Sun Inn was already almost thirty years old.

This handsome stone building, erected in a classic Moravian style, was capped by a red tile roof, which signaled travelers for miles that food and shelter were within sight. Almost every Revolutionary statesman stayed in the inn, including Washington, Hancock, Lafayette, Ethan Allen and John Adams. Over the years every president from Washington through Buchanan stayed there, and Jimmy Carter reestablished the presidential tradition.

So popular was the Sun Inn that it grew from its original two stories with attic, to three full stories (still with its signature red roof), and finally to four (with a flat roof). In the 1850s, a rear extension was added, and balconies and shops were carved into street level space along Main Street. Nineteenth-century photographs show a fine Victorian hotel.

But Victoriana was not the interest of the Sun Inn Preservation Society, formed in 1971. They were determined to bring the Sun Inn, then being threatened with demolition, back to its eighteenth-century appearance.

Now the building has been pared of its extension, stripped of its Main Street side shops, brought back to the original height and recapped in red tile. The lower floor is furnished as it would have been in the years before 1800 and is open to the public for daily guided tours.

But to keep the Sun Inn a living landmark, the second floor has been leased out as a restaurant. Here, too, you'll find a recreation of the ambience of the past. Wide plank floors topped with hooked rugs and just a select few artworks on the muted walls harken to an older time.

However, the food, while drawing from traditional American dishes, is definitely up-to-date. For example, the Conti-

146

nental Chicken Salad, served at lunch, combines diced chicken with pasta and pesto. Cornplanter's Plum Chicken, a dinner entrée, uses a trendy combination of plum and walnut sauce to enhance the chicken.

How would the Marquis de Chastellux describe twentieth-century victuals? I'm not sure, but I suspect he would find them as satisfying as those he feasted on two centuries ago.—C.W.

The Sun Inn is located at 564 Main Street in Bethlehem. Lunch is served from 11:00 a.m. until 3:00 p.m., Tuesday through Saturday. Dinner is served from 6:00 p.m. until 9:00 p.m., Wednesday and Thursday, and from 6:00 p.m. until 10:00 p.m., Friday and Saturday. Sunday brunch is served from 10:00 a.m. until 2:00 p.m. For reservations (mandatory during the Christmas season, suggested at other times) call (215) 867-1761.

SUN INN'S NEW ENGLAND STUFFED CORNISH HEN

6 **Cornish game hens**	3 **teaspoons cinnamon**
¼ **cup sweet butter**	4 **cups chicken stock**
1 **onion, finely chopped**	2 **cups long-grain rice**
2 **stalks celery, finely**	½ **cup raisins**
chopped	1 **cup Kahlúa**
½ **teaspoon chopped garlic**	2 **cups apricot jam**
½ **cup pine nuts**	**salt and pepper to taste**

Preheat oven to 400 degrees. Wash and dry hens. Place breast side up on a roasting rack and bake uncovered for 25 minutes. Remove from oven and allow to cool. Meanwhile, prepare stuffing: Melt butter in a large saucepan. Sauté onions, celery and garlic until tender. Add pine nuts, cinnamon, chicken stock, rice and raisins. Bring to a boil; then lower heat and simmer until liquid is absorbed and rice is cooked. Allow to cool. When hens and stuffing are cool enough to handle, stuff and truss the hens. Over low heat in a small saucepan, heat Kahlúa and apricot jam until jam dis-

147

solves. Season to taste with salt and pepper. Reheat the oven to 350 degrees and return the stuffed hens to the oven. Roast hens for 25 minutes, basting frequently with Kahlúa mixture. Serves 6.

SUN INN'S POTATO AND CORN CHOWDER

¼ cup sweet butter
1 medium onion, finely chopped
1 green pepper, seeded and finely chopped
½ cup flour
1 quart chicken stock
4 potatoes, washed and diced

¼ cup pimientos, finely chopped
2 12-ounce cans whole kernel corn
2 12-ounce cans creamed corn
½ teaspoon basil
salt and pepper to taste

In a large soup pot, melt butter. Sauté onion and green pepper until wilted. Stir in flour, and cook, stirring, until a thick paste is formed. Pour in chicken stock and bring to a boil. Add potatoes. Lower heat and simmer for 1 hour or until potatoes are tender. Add remaining ingredients and season to taste. Serves 6.

SUN INN'S HOUSE DRESSING

1 small onion, finely minced
1 tablespoon chopped garlic
2 tablespoons finely minced scallions or chives

1 tablespoon lemon juice
1½ teaspoons red wine vinegar
1 cup plain yogurt
½ cup mayonnaise

Mix all ingredients thoroughly. The dressing may be stored in a jar in the refrigerator for several days. Yields 2 cups.

BALLIETSVILLE INN
Ballietsville

BALLIETSVILLE INN

Culinary awards have been showered on the Ballietsville Inn like spring rain. And little wonder, for this is one of the gastronomic meccas of the Lehigh Valley. If there were an honor for longevity, this inn would surely be a contender too. The first license for the premises was issued to Paulus Balliet, an immigrant from Alsace-Lorraine, on June 22, 1746. It has operated as an inn ever since.

Paulus and his wife, the former Maria Wotring, first ran their Whitehall Inn in a primitive log house. As business grew, so did the building, which eventually passed from owner to owner. Its full genealogy is prominently displayed in the front hall of the present stone structure, a lovely building whose "new wing" dates from 1840.

The inn had its ups and downs before it was rescued by Swiss restaurateur Joseph Hartmann in 1971. Born into a Basel hotel family, he worked in Paris and Venice before going to sea as chef with the Holland–America Line. In 1961, he landed in Philadelphia, where he eventually teamed up with Richard W. Gemmel to find a restaurant.

When the partners were researching the history of the rundown inn they bought in Ballietsville, they discovered that Richard Wotring Gemmel was a descendent of Paulus and Maria. So Richard has given the present restaurant its pedigree, while Joseph has imprinted on it the stamp of French-Swiss culinary excellence. The menu, which changes seasonally, features some fine renditions of familiar dishes and some creations that are the Ballietsville Inn's own.

During my summer visit, I was seated at a round table in the cozy Emperor Room. The Viande de Grison sur Melon appetizer, featuring an exquisite Swiss air-dried beef rarely found on an American menu, would suit even a dieter. A simply but perfectly broiled fish or grilled meat would also be a good diet choice.

But why think about calories if you can persuade your partner to share a Filet de Veau Anna, a house specialty of fillet of roast veal, wrapped in bacon, and served with a truffle-studded wine sauce? Or go solo with Noisette de Porc Robert, lovely loin of pork with a fine mustard sauce. These are the light summer creations; imagine the richness of the game dishes featured in fall and winter.

From the dessert cart, which is truly art from the kitchen, I opted for an unusual version of a common dish. The Chocolate Mousse is an airy concoction which resembles a frothy hillock of white and brown marble. It looked wonderful and tasted even better.

The Ballietsville Inn is one of those restaurants where you don't go to eat. You go to dine. And splendid dining it is.—C.W.

The Ballietsville Inn is located at 60 Main Street in Ballietsville. Dinner is served from 5:30 p.m. until 10:00 p.m., Monday through Saturday, and from 4:00 p.m. until 9:00 p.m. on Sunday. For reservations (suggested) call (215) 799-2435.

BALLIETSVILLE INN'S SHRIMP DELIGHT

½ pound salted butter
3 garlic cloves, finely chopped
½ bunch parsley, finely chopped
¼ teaspoon chopped fresh basil
¼ teaspoon chopped fresh thyme
¼ teaspoon chopped fresh oregano

salt and pepper to taste
1½ pounds medium shrimp, shelled and deveined
16 to 18 canned artichoke hearts (2 14-ounce cans), quartered
1 pound Danish Fontina cheese, grated
6 slices good-quality white bread, toasted

Soften butter at room temperature. Blend the garlic, herbs, salt and pepper into the butter. Preheat oven to 350 degrees. Melt half of the butter mixture in a large skillet and sauté the shrimp for 1 minute. Spoon into 6 shallow ovenproof dishes. Divide artichoke hearts evenly among the 6 dishes. Dot with remaining butter. Cover generously with cheese. Bake until cheese is melted and bubbling, about 6 minutes. Serve with toast points. Serves 6.

151

BALLIETSVILLE INN'S NOISETTES DE PORC ROBERT

3 pork tenderloins (10 to 12 ounces each)
½ cup chopped Spanish onion
1 cup white wine
1¼ cups Brown Sauce (see index)

3 tablespoons Dijon mustard
salt and pepper to taste
oil
⅓ cup chopped parsley

Carefully trim each tenderloin, removing all of the silver membrane. In a medium saucepan, combine the onions and wine, and cook until reduced by one-half. Stir in Brown Sauce and simmer, skimming as needed. Slowly whisk in mustard and salt and pepper; continue to simmer until sauce is smooth. Meanwhile, brush tenderloins with oil and broil under medium-high heat, turning once, approximately 8 minutes on each side. To serve, slice the pork on the bias. Spoon sauce on a heated serving platter or 6 individual dinner plates, top with overlapping slices of pork and sprinkle with chopped parsley. Serves 6.

BALLIETSVILLE INN'S CHOCOLATE MOUSSE

½ pound semisweet chocolate
1 pint heavy cream
3 egg whites
1 cup sugar

4 tablespoons of semisweet chocolate bits or grated chocolate
whipped cream

Melt chocolate in the top of a double boiler over hot but not boiling water. Cool. Whip cream until stiff. Beat egg whites and sugar until stiff. Fold all ingredients together, "undermixing" so that the mixture remains white streaked with chocolate. Chill. Serve with whipped cream. Serves 6.

THE PHOEBE SNOW IN THE HILTON
AT LACKAWANNA STATION
Scranton

THE PHOEBE SNOW   I live in the town of Hoboken, whose pride is a landmark Erie-Lackawanna Terminal designed by architect Kenneth Murchison. I was delighted to learn that Scranton's Hilton at Lackawanna Station, the railroad station built when Scranton was a prosperous mining and manufacturing town, was a Murchison masterpiece, too. Ground was broken in 1906 for this grand station, designed in a French Renaissance style.

The most famous of the twelve daily passenger trains that stopped in Scranton was the Lackawanna Railroad's "Phoebe Snow." The name was invented by a clever railroad promoter to imply that the ride was clean and pleasant, a farfetched and hyperbolic notion in the days of noisy, dirty coal-fired steam engines.

Much of what nostalgic visitors now find at the old station recalls those days—happily without the noise and dirt. Antique engines and cars are permanently parked on sidings, a railroad buff's paradise known as Steamtown USA.

What was once hailed as one of the country's most beautiful railroad stations must now be ranked as one of its loveliest hotels. The Hilton was miraculously created from the old station, which has been terribly rundown even before it lay empty for twelve years. But neither time nor neglect could dim the beauty of the ornate waiting room, which is now the hotel lobby and lounge. Beneath a vaulted, leaded-glass ceiling are walls of red marble from Siena and green marble from the Alps and a floor of inlaid terrazzo. Lining the spacious room is a museum-quality series of faience panels depicting scenes along the old Lackawanna route between Hoboken and Buffalo. In one corner is the fine restaurant called The Phoebe Snow.

The offerings for each course are artfully composed, exquisitely garnished and beautifully sauced. The Salmon Stuffed with Shrimp Mousseline and Spinach en Croûte was a frothy appetizer napped in Champagne Sauce. Chicken Involtini is a fortuitous marriage of poultry, Canadian bacon and cheese under a mantle of Marsala Sauce. I sighed over the

154

selections from the dessert cart, finding it difficult to narrow my choice down to a reasonable one, or two, from the fabulous array of tortes and pastries.

An ambitious menu, crisp Continental service and a truly unique atmosphere roll back the clock to the gilded age when the original "Phoebe Snow" operated. History has perhaps come full circle, because the restaurant finally is a fulfillment of the elegance which its namesake was supposed to symbolize.—C.W.

The Hilton at Lackawanna Station is located at 700 Lackawanna Avenue in Scranton. Breakfast is served from 6:30 a.m. until 11:00 a.m., Monday through Saturday, and from 7:00 a.m. until 10:00 a.m. on Sunday. Lunch is served from 11:30 a.m. until 2:30 p.m., Monday through Saturday. Dinner is served from 5:00 p.m. until 10:00 p.m., Monday through Saturday, and from 4:00 p.m. until 10:00 p.m. on Sunday. Sunday brunch is served from 10:00 a.m. until 2:30 p.m. For reservations (suggested) call (717) 342-8300.

THE PHOEBE SNOW'S CALIFORNIA SALAD

2 artichoke hearts	2 teaspoons red wine
½ avocado	vinegar
1 tomato, peeled and seeded	salt and pepper to taste
½ pound smoked salmon	20 stalks of asparagus,
2 fresh basil leaves	peeled and cooked
20 endive spears	2 teaspoons pine nuts,
6 teaspoons olive oil	toasted lightly

Slice artichokes. Dice avocado and tomato in large chunks. Cut salmon into wide julienne strips. Cut basil leaves into very fine strips. Arrange endive in star shapes on two salad plates. Combine artichoke, avocado, tomato, salmon, basil and half of the oil, vinegar, salt and pepper. Prepare a vinaigrette of remaining oil, vinegar, salt and pepper. Spoon half of salad mixture onto center of each endive star. Dredge

155

asparagus in vinaigrette and lay onto each salad mound, alternating with endive spears. Top with pine nuts. Serves 2.

THE PHOEBE SNOW'S CHICKEN INVOLTINI

2 skinless, boneless chicken breasts (about 8 ounces each)
2 very thin slices Canadian bacon
2 very thin slices Gruyère cheese
flour
¼ cup clarified butter
Marsala Sauce (recipe below)
2 tomato skin roses
4 large mushroom caps, poached and fluted
2 large bouquets of fresh parsley

Preheat oven to 325 degrees. Lightly pound chicken breasts from the rib side. Lay slices of Canadian bacon and cheese evenly on the chicken. Roll into tight pinwheels. Dredge lightly with flour. In a medium skillet, heat clarified butter over medium-high heat. Sear the chicken, seam side first, about 30 seconds on each side. Remove chicken and place in a baking dish. Bake for 20 minutes. Place chicken on 2 dinner plates. Pour half of sauce over each portion, and garnish each with a tomato skin rose, 2 mushroom caps and a parsley bouquet. Serves 2.

Marsala Sauce:
1 tablespoon oil
1 teaspoon minced shallots
4 large mushrooms, thinly sliced
⅔ cup Marsala wine
⅔ cup Brown Sauce (see index)
pinch of thyme
salt and pepper to taste

Heat oil in a small saucepan. Lightly sauté shallots and mushrooms for one minute. Deglaze pan with Marsala. Stir in Brown Sauce and seasonings and reduce by two-thirds.

156

THE PUFFERBELLY ON
FRENCH STREET
Erie

THE PUFFERBELLY ON FRENCH STREET

Room dividers created from firefighters' lockers, a brass pole in a corner, fire company insignia, photographs of fires and the men who battled them, and a huge rescue net tacked on one wall decorate The Pufferbelly on French Street. But even without such memorabilia, it would be impossible to mistake these long, narrow rooms with their eighteen-foot ceilings for anything but an old fire station.

When the station was built in 1907, horses still drew the fire equipment. Three-quarters of a century later, when the soon-to-be restaurant required an extension in the back to accommodate a modern kitchen, landmark laws stipulated that it be designed to look like the long-demolished stable that had housed those horses. The restaurant, however, takes its name from the steam-driven pumpers and engines which soon replaced the horses.

The tables in the bar portion of The Pufferbelly are as high as the bar itself. I sat on a lofty bench along the wall during a slow period in the afternoon and sampled some of The Pufferbelly's inventive renditions of popular dishes. The chef perched on a barstool across the table from me and told me one of his true points of pride: His kitchen does not contain a fryer. He steams, he sautés, he bakes, he stir-fries and he composes— but he doesn't deep-fry anything.

Light meals, lots of seafood, super sandwiches and great salads are signatures of The Pufferbelly. The menu reflects no national borders. Will it be Potato Pancakes, served New York deli-style with apple sauce and sour cream, or a spicy Quesadilla Infierno zinged with jalapeño pepper? Sautéed Bay Scallops Scandinavian, Veal Marsala or Teriyaki Steak? The Pufferbelly offers commendable performances of an astonishing ethnic variety.

I visited when the bluefish were running, so my choice was that flavorful fish, here served with a Cajun-style topping. For some reason, fish always creates in me a craving for chocolate, which was amply satisfied with a Boule de Neige, a rich tennis ball-size hunk of chocolate decorated with whipped cream.

Satisfying cravings, whether for good food, refreshing drinks or congenial companionship, is something the Pufferbelly accomplishes in style.—c.w.

The Pufferbelly is located at 414 French Street in Erie. Meals are served from 11:00 a.m. until 10:00 p.m., Monday through Thursday, and from 11:00 a.m. until midnight, Friday and Saturday. A buffet brunch is served from 11:00 a.m. until 2:30 p.m. on Sunday, and dinner is served from 3:00 p.m. until 7:00 p.m. Sunday. For reservations (not required but accepted for dinner) call (814) 454-1557.

THE PUFFERBELLY'S TURKEY AND PEA POD QUICHE

3 eggs
1½ cups half and half
salt and pepper to taste
1 cup grated Swiss cheese
1 baked 9-inch pie shell

½ pound cooked turkey, diced
¼ pound snow pea pods, trimmed

Preheat oven to 350 degrees. Lightly beat the eggs and whisk in half and half, salt and pepper. Spread one-half of the cheese on the bottom of the pie shell. Spread the turkey over the cheese. Arrange the pea pods in a clocklike pattern over the turkey. Carefully pour the egg mixture over all. Top with remaining cheese. Bake 45 minutes or until quiche is firm and golden brown. Serve with Hollandaise Sauce (see index) or Béarnaise Sauce (commercial or homemade). Serves 6.

THE PUFFERBELLY'S CAJUN STYLE BLUEFISH

½ cup mayonnaise
3 tablespoons finely chopped green onion
3 tablespoons finely chopped parsley
3 tablespoons finely chopped dill pickle

⅛ teaspoon cayenne
1½ teaspoons Dijon-style mustard
2 pounds bluefish fillets (or other fleshy fish)
1 cup seasoned breadcrumbs

159

Mix mayonnaise, green onion, parsley, pickles, cayenne and mustard (this mixture may be prepared in advance and refrigerated). Place fillets on a lightly oiled baking sheet. Spread 1 to 2 tablespoons of the mayonnaise mixture on each fillet. Top generously with breadcrumbs. Bake at 350 degrees until fish is tender and flakey but not dried out (10 to 15 minutes depending on thickness of fillets). Serves 4 to 6.

THE PUFFERBELLY'S BOULE DE NEIGE

8 ounces dark sweet
  chocolate
½ cup strong black coffee
1 cup sugar
½ pound sweet butter,
  softened

4 eggs
1 tablespoon dark rum
whipped cream
mint leaves

In the top of a double boiler over hot water, combine the chocolate, coffee and sugar and heat until chocolate is melted. Transfer the mixture to the bowl of an electric mixer and mix at low speed, adding the butter one small chunk at a time. When thoroughly combined, add the eggs one at a time, then add rum. Pour into a 1½-quart, lightly greased baking dish and bake at 350 degrees for 55 minutes. (The top will be cracked when it is done.) Cool to room temperature and refrigerate. To serve, scoop out portions of the Boule, cover with stars of whipped cream and garnish with mint leaves. Serves 4.

EAGLE HOTEL
Waterford

EAGLE HOTEL **W**aterford is now just a wide spot along Route 19, but when the Eagle Hotel was built in 1827, it was a key resting place between Erie and Meadville, a one-day coach journey. The crest of builder Thomas King may still be seen above the third-floor windows on the side of the lovely Georgian structure, and his initials are still discernible on the wrought iron front door handle.

At one time, the Eagle Hotel had drawing rooms for genteel ladies and their gentlemen traveling companions to the left of the wide center hallway, and a tap room for rowdier men to the right. There were only four upstairs guest chambers and a dormitory for drovers, for the Eagle Hotel was a place to rest, eat and change horses rather than a usual overnight stop. Meals were prepared in a separate kitchen building, now long gone.

In 1845 an unknown hotel maid went berserk and set the Eagle Hotel aflame. The stone walls remained, but much of the interior had to be rebuilt.

When railroads replaced horsedrawn coaches, the Eagle Hotel lost its importance and went through good periods and bad, as it was sold in and out of the King family. In 1974, the last private owner died, the furnishings were auctioned off and the building was precariously positioned between demolition and salvation. But the Fort Le Boeuf Historical Society bought it in 1977, got it listed on the National Register of Historic Places, and set about saving it.

The restoration has been a labor of love on the part of a handful of dedicated volunteers. They have replaced beams and replastered walls, rebuilt mantelpieces and recaulked windows, scoured the neighborhood for appropriate furnishings and even permitted an archeological dig to be mounted in the backyard.

In 1980, starting with a Christmas dinner, society members began serving occasional meals and even issued a cookbook as a way of raising local consciousness about the building. The following summer they opened the Eagle Hotel for informal and inexpensive weekend dinners.

162

Now visitors sit at age-scarred tables, peer through the small panes of nine-over-nine windows, and select from an ever-changing menu of light lunches or simple dinners. They usually top it with a special dessert from a historic society member's repertoire, knowing that every bite is for a good cause.—C.W.

The Eagle Hotel is located at 22 High Street in Waterford. It is open from 11:00 a.m. until 8:00 p.m., Saturday and Sunday. Luncheon selections are offered through mid- to late afternoon, when there is a transition to the dinner menu. For reservations (accepted but not necessary) call (814) 796-6990.

EAGLE HOTEL'S NAVY BEAN SOUP

1 pound dried navy beans
3 quarts water
1 ham bone with meat
2 stalks celery, chopped
1 medium onion, chopped
1 carrot, peeled and
  chopped

1 bay leaf
1 teaspoon thyme
1 tablespoon Worcestershire
  sauce
salt and pepper to taste

Wash beans in a large pot, drain and cover with water. Soak beans overnight and then bring to a boil, or bring water to a simmer for two minutes, then let stand for 1 hour. Then proceed with recipe by adding ham bone, chopped vegetables and bay leaf. Reduce heat to a simmer and cook, uncovered, 3 to 4 hours, until beans are soft. Remove ham bone and bay leaf. With a wooden spoon, mash beans against the side and bottom of the pot. Cut meat off the bone, chop and add to soup along with thyme and Worcestershire sauce. Season to taste with salt and pepper. Serves 12.

EAGLE HOTEL'S CHICKEN IN WINE SAUCE

2 to 4 tablespoons sweet
  butter
4 whole chicken breasts,
  split, skinned and boned

1 10¾-ounce can of
  condensed cream of mushroom soup
⅔ cup Chablis

163

Melt butter in a large saucepan and sauté chicken breasts on both sides until lightly browned. Mix soup and Chablis and pour over chicken. Cover and simmer for one hour. Serves 8.

EAGLE HOTEL'S FROSTY LEMON CREAM PIE

Graham Cracker Crust:

1½ cups crushed graham crackers

⅓ cup sweet butter or margarine, melted

¼ cup sugar

Blend ingredients and pat into a 9-inch pie plate, reserving 2 tablespoons of crumbs for topping. Bake in a 375-degree oven for 8 to 10 minutes. Cool and fill.

Filling:

½ cup sugar
⅓ cup undiluted frozen lemonade concentrate
1 egg white

3 to 4 drops yellow food coloring
1 cup heavy cream
1 Graham Cracker Crust

Combine sugar, lemonade and egg white, and beat at high speed until thickened (about 3 to 5 minutes). Carefully fold in food coloring. Whip cream until stiff and gently fold into lemonade mixture. Spoon into baked, cooled crust. Sprinkle with reserved crumbs. Freeze until firm (4 to 6 hours). Yields 1 pie.

NOTE: This recipe, doubled, will serve 15 when prepared in a 9- by 13-inch pan. In this case, place crust only in the bottom of the pan, and serve dessert cut into squares.

HOTEL CONNEAUT
Conneaut Lake

HOTEL CONNEAUT   The Hotel Conneaut was built in 1892 as a thousand-room resort on the shore of Pennsylvania's largest natural body of water. It suffered a disastrous fire just sixteen years later. Only one wing of the huge white frame structure survived—and that wing is still operating as the Hotel Conneaut.

The hotel and its surrounding land were originally owned by the Pittsburgh, Shenango and Lake Erie Railroad, which built an amusement park and, to fill it with merrymakers, a railroad station with enough sidings to accommodate eight trains simultaneously.

Even after the motorcar replaced the train, and the Depression saw the resort complex sink into receivership, Conneaut Lake Park remained a popular summer excursion destination. Families from Pittsburgh to Erie continued flocking to the rides and the beach, while young adults danced the night away at the park's Dreamland Ballroom, the largest clear-span dance hall between New York and Chicago. Bandleader Freddy Carlone gave a young hotel barber the opportunity to sing with the band. Carlone's name is now a footnote to musical history, but the young barber, Perry Como, went on to superstardom.

Three prominent families from nearby Meadville bailed the park out of bankruptcy. One of them, the Flynn family, now owns it and continues to operate it as a family resort, with such amusement park staples as a rumbling wooden roller coaster, a bright midway, a carousel with horses carved of real wood and a tame Kiddieland.

The hotel, now pared to a cozy 132 rooms, is also a casual family place. The dining room on the ground floor, with a lovely lake view, rambles comfortably through arches and into alcoves, and there is a pleasant glassed-in porch overlooking the grounds.

The food is geared to families—famlies with hearty appetites. The most popular dinners are from the family-style dinner menu, featuring all-you-can-eat entrées.

I had to tear myself away from the bread basket, packed

with an assortment of wonderful breads, rolls and muffins, to try the Country Fried Steak, a hefty chunk of flavorful beef sautéed with onions and green peppers and in a rich brown gravy. I also sampled the Creamy Seafood Fettucini and found it as rich as its name implies.

Smart diners leave some room for dessert. I was not surprised to learn that the chef who devised the baked goods recipes has been lured away to become the pastry chef at a major hotel in Germany. Although the Hotel Conneaut will miss her, the Flynns promise that her recipes will remain.—c.w.

The Hotel Conneaut, located at Conneaut Lake Park, is open from Memorial Day through Labor Day. In the dining room, breakfast is served from 8:00 a.m. until noon, Monday through Friday, and from 7:30 a.m. until noon, Saturday and Sunday. Lunch is served from noon until 2:00 p.m., daily except Sunday. Sunday brunch is served from 10:00 a.m. until 2:00 p.m. Dinner is served from 5:00 p.m. until 10:00 p.m., nightly. For reservations call (814) 382-5165.

HOTEL CONNEAUT'S PEPPERONI ROLLS

2 tablespoons sugar
1 teaspoon salt
1½ tablespoons oil
2 egg yolks
½ cup water
1¼ tablespoon yeast
¼ cup warm water

2¾ cups bread flour
¼ pound pepperoni, finely
    chopped
3 ounces Provolone cheese,
    shredded
½ stick sweet butter, melted

Combine sugar, salt, oil, egg yolks and ½ cup water; mix well. Meanwhile, dissolve yeast in ¼ cup warm water and set aside to proof. Sift flour and add to dry ingredients. By hand or in a mixer (at medium speed) fitted with a dough hook, knead dough for about 10 minutes. Turn dough into a well-greased bowl, cover with a towel and set aside in a warm place until double in bulk (about 1 hour). Punch dough down and turn out onto a lightly floured board.

167

Pinch off pieces of dough about the size of golf balls. Shape each dough ball into a flat oval shape. Combine pepperoni and cheese and sprinkle a small amount of this mixture on each dough oval. Roll mixture into dough. Place dough ovals 2 to 2½ inches apart on cookie sheets covered with a sheet of baking parchment. Cover and set aside in a warm place until doubled in bulk. Brush with melted butter and bake at 375 degrees until brown (about 8 minutes). Yields 18 to 20 rolls.

HOTEL CONNEAUT'S CREAMY SEAFOOD FETTUCINI

¼ pound scallops
¼ pound crabmeat
2 tablespoons olive oil
¼ pound cooked spinach
  fettucini
½ cup half and half
⅔ cup Ricotta cheese

1 cup Parmesan cheese,
  grated
½ teaspoon crushed red
  pepper
¼ teaspoon garlic powder
salt and pepper to taste

In a skillet over medium heat, sauté scallops and crabmeat in olive oil until heated through. Drain liquid from pan. Add fettucini and stir until heated. Stir in half and half, Ricotta and Parmesan and cook, stirring, until sauce thickens (about 3 minutes). Season to taste with crushed red pepper, garlic powder, salt and pepper. Yields 2 entrée servings or 3 to 4 appetizers.

NOTE: One clove of fresh garlic, peeled and minced, may be substituted for garlic powder; it should be sautéed with the scallops and crabmeat.

HOTEL CONNEAUT'S HERSHEY BAR PIE

12 ounces semisweet
  chocolate
1 cup milk

36 large marshmallows
2 cups heavy cream
2 baked 9-inch pie shells

Combine chocolate, milk and marshmallows in a saucepan over medium heat and stir until chocolate and marshmallows melt. Chill. Whip heavy cream until stiff. Fold into chocolate-marshmallow mixture and pour half of mixture into each baked shell. Yields 2 pies.

CHESTNUT STREET STATION
Meadville

CHESTNUT STREET STATION

When the old Erie Railroad was headquartered in Meadville, and other trains also came through, the town was an important rail center. There were four thousand railroad jobs, and numerous passenger and freight trains stopped every day. In honor of this tradition, and to attract the region's many railroad buffs, Bob Winters gave the name Chestnut Street Station to the restaurant he created in 1985 from the old Hirsch Brothers dry-goods store. This corner building at Meadville's main downtown intersection dates from the 1890s, and while Winters has somewhat modernized the storefront, he has kept a number of the enchanting old decorative touches inside and added others.

The restaurant manages to be at once contemporary and traditional. Old-style tongue-and-groove wainscoting comes in a modern light-hued poplar. The original pressed-tin ceiling remains, and on the narrow balconies overlooking the dining area are scattered individual antiques, plus dioramas on town and country themes.

Railroad memorabilia, of course, appear among the decorative accents. My favorite is the New York Central Railroad conductor's cap perched rakishly atop Mr. Moosie, the huge stuffed moose head that presides over the very tiny ice cream bar just inside the main entrance. Mr. Moosie is impossible to miss, nor should the ice cream treats whose preparations he observes be passed over. The Chestnut Street Station makes wondrous sundaes and shakes with improbably rich Pennsylvania ice cream—an eighteen percent butterfat blend.

It's a good thing that my companion and I had selected a reasonably light lunch before we dipped into dessert. We ordered three light luncheon entrées, split them between us, and nibbled discreetly. Chestnut Street Station has shared recipes for all three. If I had a home ice cream freezer, I would be tempted to try reproducing the desserts as well, but since I don't, I suppose I'll have to make another pilgrimage to Meadville.—C.W.

170

Chestnut Street Station is located at 257 Chestnut Street in Meadville. Breakfast, lunch and daily specials are served from 7:00 a.m. until 3:00 p.m. on Monday; from 7:00 a.m. until 7:00 p.m. Tuesday through Friday; and from 11:00 a.m. until 7:00 p.m. on Saturday. For reservations (recommended on weekends) call (814) 337-5081.

CHESTNUT STREET STATION'S
ENCHANTFUL ALMOND SALAD

1 chicken breast, boned and skinned

½ cup fresh pineapple chunks

½ cup mandarin orange sections

2 cups mixed salad greens, washed

¼ cup slivered almonds, toasted

Dressing (recipe below)

Poach chicken breast gently in lightly salted water to cover, about 25 minutes. When cool enough to handle, pull into bite-sized chunks. Allow to cool to room temperature. Mix chicken, pineapple and oranges. Arrange salad greens on a platter. Top with chicken and fruit mixture. Sprinkle with almonds and pour Dressing over. Serves 2 as an entrée or 4 as an appetizer.

Dressing:

1 package instant vanilla pudding

orange extract

Prepare pudding according to package directions, but use twice the quantity of liquid called for. Flavor ½ cup with orange extract to taste.

CHESTNUT STREET STATION'S
VEGETARIAN DELIGHT

2 to 3 cups assorted fresh vegetables (your choice)

2 large slices good-quality bread

2 large slices Monterey Jack cheese, ¼ inch thick

¼ cup alfalfa sprouts

171

Steam vegetables (separately if necessary) until cooked through but still crisp. Drain. Meanwhile, place bread slices on 2 flameproof plates. Top with vegetable mixture and cheese. Place under broiler or heat in microwave oven until cheese is melted. Top with alfalfa sprouts and serve immediately. Serves 2.

CHESTNUT STREET STATION'S CRAB CAKES

1 pound crabmeat
¼ cup chopped green
   pepper
¼ cup chopped onion
1 teaspoon lemon juice
1 teaspoon paprika
½ teaspoon Worcestershire
   sauce
salt and pepper to taste
1 cup unseasoned
   breadcrumbs

2 eggs, beaten
flour
3 tablespoons butter
4 thin slices good-quality
   bread
1 large ripe tomato, seeded
   and diced
4 slices Monterey Jack
   cheese

Mix crabmeat with next 8 ingredients. Form into 4 patties. Sprinkle with flour and sauté in melted butter, first browning quickly on both sides and then cooking over lowered heat 5 to 6 minutes. Place bread slices on flameproof plates. Top each with 2 cooked crab cakes. Sprinkle with diced tomato. Place cheese on top and broil or place in microwave until cheese has melted. Serves 4.

HYEHOLDE RESTAURANT
Coraopolis-Moon Township

HYEHOLDE
RESTAURANT

What a romantic place the Hyeholde Restaurant is. This Tudor mansion combines the rugged masculinity of medieval-style rooms—beamed ceilings, huge fireplaces, wrought iron chandeliers and antique tapestries—with softer details such as fresh flowers, custom-made Staffordshire service plates and flattering lighting.

The Hyeholde comes by its romantic ambience naturally. It was created by William Kryskill to fulfill a promise to his adored wife, Clara, that he would build her a castle. The Kryskills, who had run a summer tearoom in Noank, Connecticut, built the Hyeholde together between 1933 and 1940, and together they operated a restaurant there.

In 1974, Pittsburgh pub owner Pat Foy bought the Hyeholde. He moved his family into the upstairs apartment and began reshaping the restaurant according to his dreams, much as Bill Kryskill had created it to realize his own.

Some years later, as the Mobil Travel Guide reviewer was dining in the Great Hall, Rex, the Foys' German Shepherd, pushed open the front door, sauntered through the dining room and mounted the stairs to the apartment. He then climbed onto a small balcony, put his paws on the railing and looked down on the reviewer. Fortunately, the reviewer either didn't notice Rex's visit or chose to overlook it, for the Hyeholde received Mobil's top four-star rating.

It's no wonder. Were I that reviewer, not even a flock of shepherds would have deterred me from showering stars on the exquisite Hyeholde and its kitchen. Quality tells from the first nibble of the home-baked breads. As a starter with those breads, I selected Hyeholde's Famous Sherry Bisque, the only Kryskill culinary legacy that still appears on the parchment menu.

Picking an entrée proved my most difficult decision. Would it be Chicken Hyeholde, a breast of chicken stuffed with apples and chestnuts and topped with a sauce velouté? Or perhaps the popular Rack of Lamb Persillade?

To leave room for dessert, I finally selected Virginia Spots, a local delicacy. The Hyeholde's version consists of two fillets of Chesapeake Bay black bass, dipped in parsley-seasoned crumbs, lightly oven-sautéed and napped with Hollandaise. I ended my glorious feast with a superb cold soufflé, a velvety citron concoction topped with warm orange sauce.

The Hyeholde is a place to toast someone special with vintage champagne, to flirt, to fall in love—or to fall in love again.—c.w.

The Hyeholde Restaurant is located on Coraopolis Heights Road in Moon Township, just outside Coraopolis. Lunch is served from 11:30 a.m. until 2:00 p.m., Wednesday and Thursday. Dinner is served from 5:00 p.m. until 10:00 p.m., Monday through Saturday. For reservations (required) call (412) 264-3116.

HYEHOLDE RESTAURANT'S FAMOUS SHERRY BISQUE

1 small ham hock
¾ cup split peas
1 small bay leaf
6 cups beef stock (commercial or homemade)
¼ cup ground salt pork
¾ cup diced onion
½ cup diced celery

2½ tablespoons flour
1 cup tomato purée
1¼ cups hot chicken stock
¼ cup dry sherry
¼ cup sweet butter
fresh ground pepper to taste
salt to taste

Place ham hock, split peas, bay leaf and 4 cups beef stock in a 4-quart pot. Bring to a boil, then reduce heat and simmer. In a separate saucepan, sauté salt pork until some of the fat is rendered. Add onion and celery, and cook until nearly tender, stirring occasionally. Stir in flour to make a roux, and cook for 5 to 6 minutes. Gradually add remaining beef stock, stirring until slightly thickened and smooth. Combine with ham and pea mixture, and simmer for 1 to 1½ hours, until peas are soft. Remove ham hock and bay leaf, and purée remaining mixture in a food mill. Place in a large saucepan. Add tomato purée and hot chicken stock, and heat over a low flame. Add sherry and butter, stirring until butter is melted. Season with

175

fresh ground pepper and salt to taste. Strain before serving. Serves 12.

HYEHOLDE RESTAURANT'S LINGUINE GRAND PARMA

1 pound linguine noodles
¼ cup sweet butter
½ pound lobster meat, diced
½ pound prosciutto ham, diced

1 cup heavy cream
½ cup grated Parmesan cheese
fresh ground pepper to taste

Cook linguine noodles in boiling salted water according to package instructions until *al dente,* and drain. Meanwhile, melt butter in a skillet and add lobster meat. Cook until the lobster becomes firm. Add prosciutto and cook for a few minutes more. Add cream and Parmesan, and continue to cook, stirring constantly, until the sauce thickens. Stir in drained linguine. Season to taste with pepper. Stir with a fork to coat linguine with sauce, and serve immediately. Serves 4.

HYEHOLDE RESTAURANT'S VIRGINIA SPOTS

2 pounds boneless, skinless Chesapeake black bass (or striped bass) fillets
½ cup vegetable oil
2 cups fresh breadcrumbs
2 tablespoons chopped parsley

salt and pepper to taste
2 to 3 tablespoons sweet butter
½ cup water
Hollandaise Sauce (see index)

Preheat oven to 350 degrees. Toss fillets in oil until they are well coated. Mix breadcrumbs and parsley, and season to taste with salt and pepper. Remove fillets from oil and lightly roll them in the seasoned crumbs. Shake off excess crumbs and place fillets on a baking sheet with a rim. Dot with butter. Pour ½ cup water on the sheet around the fish and bake for 20 to 30 minutes or until fish flakes easily. Serve with Hollandaise Sauce. Serves 4.

GRAND CONCOURSE
Pittsburgh

GRAND CONCOURSE The beautiful Beaux Arts Pittsburgh & Lake Erie terminal on the banks of the Monongahela River is the kind of palatial public space that, in less enlightened times, America used to demolish. The same fate could have befallen this Pittsburgh landmark, which had been vacant for nearly a decade. Fortunately, the magnificent 1901 terminal fell into the hands of Chuck Muer, a visionary who has made a career of restoring old buildings around the country and converting them into restaurants.

The terminal's square gray facade hides a glittering interior capped by a vaulted, stained-glass ceiling. During World War II, the glass was painted over as part of the blackout. No one has ever counted how many gallons of oven cleaner were needed to restore the ceiling, but the effort was worthwhile, for having lunch or brunch in the cathedral-size main dining room (formerly the main concourse) is like eating inside a crystal or a diamond.

I passed the main dining room, the crowded and lively Gandy Dancer Saloon (once the ticket office) and the Oyster Bar (formerly the baggage-claim room) on my way to lunch in the River Room, a glassed-in former loading dock with a grand view of the skyline, the river and the century-old Smithfield Street Bridge.

Charley's Chowder, a tomato-based fish soup, is an obligatory start for each Grand Concourse meal. I followed it with Seafood Pasta Pagliara, a toothsome mix of linquine, shellfish and spinach. Had I been in the mood for straight seafood, I'd have ordered Charley's Bucket, a generous clambake consisting of a whole Maine lobster, Dungeness crab, mussels, clams, corn on the cob and boiled redskin potatoes.

I was enchanted by the restaurant's clever attention to detail. Menus are displayed where train bulletins once were posted. Banquettes in the main dining room were made to resemble old railroad station benches, although they are considerably more comfortable. The dessert menu appears on an old conductor's ring; to order, you pull off the sweet that suits you and hand the ticket to the waiter or waitress. I requested the Minted Sundae, but I was also intrigued by my companion's Strawberries and Pepper.

The P.&L.E. terminal reflected not only what has been called America's Gilded Age, but also the golden era of its railroads, when the well-to-do lived, traveled and dined in luxury. They made no apologies for extravagance in architecture—or anything else. Isn't it a treat to be able to sample such lavishness in our own high-tech time?—C.W.

The Grand Concourse is located between the Smithfield Street Bridge and the Station Square shopping mall on the southern bank of the Monongahela River in Pittsburgh. Lunch is served from 11:30 a.m. until 2:30 p.m., Monday through Friday. Sunday brunch is served from 10:00 a.m. until 2:30 p.m. Dinner is served from 5:00 p.m. until 10:00 p.m., Monday through Thursday; from 5:00 p.m. until 11:00 p.m., Friday and Saturday; and from 5:00 p.m. until 9:00 p.m. on Sunday. The Gandy Dancer Saloon serves drinks and food throughout the day and stays open later than the dining rooms. For reservations (recommended) call (412) 261-1717.

GRAND CONCOURSE'S CHARLEY'S CHOWDER

4 tablespoons olive oil
2 medium garlic cloves, crushed
¼ cup finely chopped onion
pinch of basil
pinch of oregano
pinch of thyme
⅓ cup finely chopped celery
¾ cup finely chopped stewed tomatoes
6 cups clam juice
1 pound boneless fish (pollack or turbot)
salt to taste
1 tablespoon finely chopped fresh parsley

In a large pot, heat olive oil. Add garlic and cook, stirring to prevent burning, until golden. With a spoon, remove garlic. Add onions and sauté, stirring frequently for 1 to 2 minutes. Add basil, oregano and thyme and cook another minute. Add celery and sauté until translucent. Add tomatoes and reduce

179

heat. Cover and simmer for 20 to 25 minutes, stirring frequently to prevent sticking or burning. Add clam juice and fish. Raise heat and cook uncovered for 15 minutes. Add salt, cover, reduce heat to low and simmer for 20 minutes, stirring often to break fish into chunks. Garnish with chopped parsley. Serves 8.

GRAND CONCOURSE'S STRAWBERRIES AND PEPPER

1 pound fresh whole strawberries, hulled
1 tablespoon coarse ground black pepper
4 tablespoons sugar
4 teaspoons Grand Marnier
4 teaspoons Pernod
1 fresh papaya or cantaloupe
4 tablespoons heavy cream
fresh mint

In a mixing bowl, gently mix strawberries, pepper and sugar. Add Grand Marnier and Pernod and gently toss. Cut papaya or cantaloupe into quarters, leaving one corner of each quarter attached. Remove peel and gently press quarters down to create a fan effect. Place papaya or melon on a plate, top with strawberry mixture and pour heavy cream over fruit. Garnish with a sprig of mint. Serves 4.

ARTHUR'S
Pittsburgh

ARTHUR'S

I approached Arthur's on foot, crossing the stark, contemporary plaza of the PPG corporate office complex. Imagine my surprise when a soft buff-colored Greek Revival facade nudged into view between two hard-edged towers of glass and steel. It was the Burke Building. Designed in 1836 by John Chislett, Pittsburgh's first major architect, it is considered one of the finest buildings of its type in America. My delight at finding this treasure turned into joy when I noticed that this was the restaurant I was seeking.

At the bar inside, I was astonished to see what looked like row after row of the same whiskey. Then I saw that the white lettering on the black labels identified dozens of different Scotch distilleries. Owner Chuck Liberatore, who created Arthur's in 1977, told me that his restaurant boasts the largest selection of Scotch whiskey in the world. The rarest bottle of Scotch was unearthed by Rommel in the desert. That's a museum piece to admire; there are plenty of other Scotches to drink. There are one hundred and ten distilleries in Scotland, and Arthur's stocks the nectar produced by one hundred and nine of them—two hundred varieties altogether, because some distilleries' output from different years are represented, like vintage wines.

There's more than whiskey at Arthur's. Breakfast and lunch are popular with the Pittsburgh business community, and dinner is an elegant treat. Arthur's also does a considerable business in fancy takeout (Gourmet Picnics for Friends and Lovers in summer and Fireside Feasts in winter). But I stayed inside to sample the fare in this old office building, former stock exchange, ex-bank headquarters and almost outpost of the Playboy Club before Liberatore liberated it into a classy eating place.

Of several dining areas, I like the Hickory Room best. Since the Burke Building went up when Andrew Jackson was president, this room is a tribute to Old Hickory. There are portraits of the seventh president, his family and his home.

Arthur's has something for everyone: great drinks, scrumptious soups, excellent entrées and sinful desserts. I

182

enjoyed the rich German Onion Beer Soup, a delicious change from the usual French rendition. Omelet Eduardo, from the breakfast menu, is a successful duet of eggs and shellfish. Another tempting luncheon dish is Chicken Lesja, a batter-dipped chicken breast sautéed with capers, mushrooms and white wine.

The more formal dinner offerings include several entrées of veal, shrimp and fresh fish. Had I had dinner instead of lunch at Arthur's, I probably would have selected the Veal ala Liberatore, because the dish that the chef names after the owner is often the finest house creation.—C.W.

Arthur's is located at 209 Fourth Avenue in Pittsburgh. Breakfast is served from 7:00 a.m. until 9:30 a.m., Monday through Friday and lunch from 11:30 a.m. until 2:30 p.m., Monday through Friday. Dinner is served from 5:30 p.m. until 10:00 p.m., Monday through Saturday. For reservations (required) call (412) 566-1735.

ARTHUR'S HOT APPLE TODDY

Hot Spiced Cider:

64 ounces pure, unsweetened apple cider
4 whole cloves

2 large cinnamon sticks
1 lemon, halved

In a saucepan, combine all the ingredients, squeezing the lemon juice into the mixture and adding both lemon halves to the pot; heat to near boiling. Strain, discarding solids. Keep filtered liquid warm until ready to serve. Yields 8 cups, enough for 8 toddies.

8 ounces Hot Spiced Cider
1 teaspoon sweet butter
1 ounce brandy
1 ounce dark rum
½ cinnamon stick

1 piece lemon rind, about 1 inch long
⅛ section of fresh apple, cored but unpeeled

For each drink, mix the Hot Spiced Cider, butter, brandy and rum. Pour into a warmed 12-ounce mug. Garnish with cinnamon stick, lemon rind and apple slice. Serve immediately. Serves 1.

ARTHUR'S OMELET EDUARDO

2 whole large shrimp,
  peeled and deveined
3 eggs
3 tablespoons sweet butter
2 ounces fresh bay scallops
2 ounces fresh crab claw
  meat, removed from shell

1 scallion, both white and
  green parts, thinly sliced
⅛ of a sweet red pepper,
  diced

Cut shrimp into ½-inch pieces; set aside. Beat eggs and set aside. Melt butter in an omelet pan. Add shrimp and sauté, stirring, until shrimp begins to turn pink. Add scallops and the crab claw meat. Continue sautéing and stirring until scallops begin to turn white. Add scallions and red pepper and continue sautéing and stirring until the vegetables begin to wilt. Pour eggs over the seafood mixture and cook until eggs are set. Serves 1.

ARTHUR'S HERITAGE PIE

1 pound sweet butter
2 large eggs
7 ounces sugar
1 teaspoon almond extract
1 ounce Amaretto di
  Saronno

1 teaspoon vanilla extract
1 graham cracker pie shell
  (see index)
whipped cream

Soften butter to room temperature. Beat eggs and sugar until lemon-colored. Mix in almond extract, Amaretto and vanilla extract and blend thoroughly. Beat in softened butter, again blending thoroughly. Pour filling into the prepared pie shell and chill until filling is firm. Garnish with whipped cream. Yields 1 pie.

THE TERRACE ROOM
THE WILLIAM PENN HOTEL
Pittsburgh

THE TERRACE ROOM
WILLIAM PENN HOTEL

In the early years of this century, when Pittsburgh symbolized the might of industrial America, the city boasted five great hotels. Only The William Penn, opened in 1916 and inextricably linked with Pittsburgh's history, remains.

The headliners who played the now-demolished Nixon Theatre, which was once across the street, stayed at The William Penn. In fact, Bob Hope proposed to his wife, Delores, there. The splendid Art Deco–style Urban Room was furnished in 1929 by theatrical designer Joseph Urban, who did many of Flo Ziegfeld's lavish stage shows..

The hotel was always full during World War II, when the nation was constantly called on to meet assorted emergencies. During the shellac shortage, The William Penn staged a dance starring the famous Sammy Kaye Orchestra. Admission was five 78 r.p.m. records. The response was so great that disks filled the lobby and the seventeenth floor, and the dancers spilled out onto the street.

Those heady war years are now four decades into history, and in the intervening years, the hotel changed hands too often and was for a time threatened with demolition. But today The William Penn, under Westin management, is once again as elegant as its designer envisioned it. The original lobby, where generations of Pittsburghers have rendezvoused, is a palm court restored right down—or up—to the ceiling, copied from the Fontainebleau Palace near Paris.

When I stayed at the hotel, I breakfasted in the Terrace Room, which I hadn't originally planned to include in this book. But I was so taken by the spaciousness and graciousness of it all that I loosened my belt for another meal. I returned for lunch, where I started with a divine, sparkling gold Chilled Consommé with Vegetables Julienne and Truffles. An exquisite main course of Beef Tips Boursin was accompanied by artful and delicious vegetables—both simple (perfectly done Green Beans) and composed (light yet rich Carrot Mousse–Stuffed Artichoke Bottoms). When it came time for dessert, I had the sense to opt for the fresh fruit selection.

The Terrace Room is everything a great hotel's main dining room should be. An unimaginably high ceiling is overhead, and lush carpeting is underfoot. Massive chandeliers cast a soft, flattering glow that makes the huge room intimate. The tables are spacious, and the armchairs are comfortable enough to invite lingering.

This classic hotel has not only survived the vagaries of nearly six decades, but has come back as an elegant landmark from a bygone era that translates beautifully to the present.—c.w.

The William Penn Hotel is located on Mellon Square in downtown Pittsburgh. The Terrace Room is open for breakfast Monday through Saturday from 7:30 a.m. until 10:30 a.m., and on Sunday from 7:30 a.m. until 10:00 a.m. Lunch is served from 11:30 a.m. until 2:30 p.m., Monday through Saturday. A short luncheon menu is available from 2:30 p.m. until 5:00 p.m., Monday through Saturday. Sunday brunch is served from 10:00 a.m. until 2:00 p.m. Dinner is served from 5:00 p.m. until 11:00 p.m., seven nights a week. Reservations are not required, but the telephone number is (412) 553-5235.

THE TERRACE ROOM'S BEEF TIPS BOURSIN

1¼ pounds tenderloin tips, sliced
salt and pepper to taste
2 tablespoons salad oil
2 tablespoons sweet butter
2 tablespoons diced shallots
1 pint heavy cream

4 tablespoons Boursin cheese, softened
2 cups spinach leaves, washed and stemmed
2 tomatoes, peeled, seeded and diced

Season tenderloin tips with salt and pepper. In a 12-inch skillet, heat the oil over medium-high heat. Add meat and brown evenly on all sides. Remove from pan and keep warm. Reduce heat to medium and add butter to pan. When butter is melted, but not burned, add shallots and sauté, stirring, until

187

golden brown. Add cream and bring to a boil. Cook, stirring frequently, until liquid is reduced by half. Stir in Boursin cheese, spinach and tomatoes. Reduce and simmer, uncovered, for 3 minutes. Put the meat back in the skillet and simmer for 2 more minutes. Serves 4.

THE TERRACE ROOM'S CARROT MOUSSE–STUFFED ARTICHOKE BOTTOMS

¾ pound carrots, peeled
  and sliced
1 cup heavy cream
2 whole cloves
½-inch cinnamon stick

1 whole egg
salt and pepper
6 artichoke bottoms
2 tablespoons clarified
  butter

Boil carrots in water to cover until tender. Drain. Preheat oven to 375 degrees. In a small saucepan, place carrots, heavy cream, cloves and cinnamon. Simmer until sauce is reduced by two-thirds and is very thick. Remove cloves and cinnamon stick; place carrots and sauce in a food processor fitted with a steel blade. Add egg; purée. Taste for seasoning, and add salt and pepper to taste if desired. Trim the bottoms of the artichokes so that they are level and place on a lightly oiled baking sheet. Put carrot mixture into a pastry bag and pipe onto artichoke bottoms as rosettes. Sprinkle with clarified butter. Bake for 15 minutes. Serves 6.

MARIO'S SOUTH SIDE SALOON
Pittsburgh

MARIO'S SOUTH SIDE SALOON

Ask a partying Pittsburgher what Mario's is famous for, and you'll be told about the great mixed drinks, about the bar's determination to keep the city's reputation as the capital of the Boilermaker going and about beer by the yard. Mario's has enrolled more than four hundred people in its First Down Club. Membership is achieved by quaffing ten yards of beer—by the yard, by the half-yard or by the foot, from vessels that all look like giant, wide-mouthed test tubes. The requirement for the Touchdown Club is the consumption of one hundred yards of beer.

Most of the appeal of this lively pub on Pittsburgh's resurgent South Side lies in the convivial atmosphere, which draws everyone from yuppies to hardhats. Contributing to the charm is the look of the place. There is a high, pressed-tin ceiling, lots of glass and lots of brass, and mellow woodwork. Closer inspection reveals the building's origins. The deep, narrow corner building, built around the turn of the century, was formerly Woshner's Haberdashery.

The glass cabinets behind the bar once held clothing on the mezzanine-level balcony, the three-ton safe on that balcony is original and the light fixture in the front window has been there as long as anyone can remember. In fact, many of Mario's male customers recall being taken, often under protest, to Woshner's for their first suits. Now the same building is, for many, the hangout of choice.

Mario's serves commendable casual food. The Texas Style Chili, Wings & Hot Sauce, Tater Skins with Cheese and Nachos & Cheese make terrific starters and great bar fare. The sandwiches and burgers at lunch are generous, and the Italian-accented dinner offerings are excellent and, in many cases, unusual.

The richest variety is the pasta selection, which consists of homemade egg or spinach fettucini topped with one of nine basic sauces and, if you wish, a mix-and-match choice of mushrooms, meatballs, sausage or seafood. I liked the Florentine Sauce, a rich amalgam of cheese, cream, spinach and bacon, but I loved the Gorgonzola Sauce, a heady three-

190

cheese mixture. And Mario's Linguine Pie, served with Caesar Salad, is a real treat for card-carrying pasta fiends.

On Friday and Saturday nights, and on Sundays after a Steelers game, Mario's opens three simple yet cozy upstairs dining rooms, which had been the Woshners' apartment when the family lived above the store. They feature such late Victorian architectural details as pocket doors and a wooden mantel flanked by beveled-glass cabinet doors. The upstairs is inviting, but so is the downstairs, where conviviality reigns seven days a week.—c.w.

Mario's is located at 1514 East Carson Street in Pittsburgh. Meals are served Monday through Saturday from 11:00 a.m. until midnight, and Sunday from 1:00 p.m. unil 10:00 p.m. For reservations (required for groups of six or more) call (412) 381-5610.

MARIO'S KIWI DAIQUIRI

1 kiwi, peeled
¾ ounce Midori liqueur
1 tablespoon powdered
  sugar

2 ounces cocktail mix
2 cups crushed ice
1 strawberry

Combine all ingredients except strawberry in a blender until thoroughly mixed. Serve in a cocktail glass garnished with a strawberry. Serves 1.

MARIO'S GORGONZOLA SAUCE

2 tablespoons sweet butter
1½ medium onions, diced
3 cups heavy cream
6 ounces Gorgonzola
  cheese, crumbled

12 ounces cream cheese,
  chunked
¼ cup grated Parmesan
  cheese

In a saucepan, melt butter and sauté onions, stirring to prevent burning. Meanwhile, in a separate saucepan, heat

191

cream (do not boil). When onions are wilted, add Gorgonzola and cook until cheese is completely melted, stirring to prevent burning. Add hot cream and mix well. Bring to a boil. Add cream cheese. Simmer until cream cheese dissolves. Stir in grated Parmesan. Sauce may be prepared in advance and carefully reheated in a saucepan. Yields enough sauce for 8 to 10 servings of pasta.

MARIO'S LINGUINE PIE

2 eggs, lightly beaten
½ cup grated Parmesan cheese
1 stick sweet butter, melted and cooled
¼ pound cooked linguine (approximately)
1 tablespoon oil
¼ medium onion, diced
½ green pepper, seeded and diced

¼ pound ground meat
1 egg, lightly beaten
1 cup Ricotta cheese
1 cup shredded Mozzarella cheese
1 tablespoon basil
1 tablespoon oregano
1 cup tomato sauce (approximately)
¼ pound pepperoni, thinly sliced

Preheat oven to 350 degrees. Mix 2 eggs, ¼ cup Parmesan, butter and linguine. Spread in the bottom of a 9-inch pie pan. In a skillet, heat oil and lightly sauté onion and green pepper until vegetables begin to soften. Add meat and brown, stirring to break up chunks. Pour off accumulated fat. Mix remaining egg, Ricotta, remaining Parmesan, ½ cup Mozzarella and herbs; set aside. Spread meat mixture on linguine layer. Top with ¼ to ½ cup tomato sauce. Add Ricotta mixture. Top with remaining tomato sauce, remaining Mozzarella and pepperoni. Bake for 20 minutes. Serves 6.

FROGGY'S
Pittsburgh

FROGGY'S

Rarely in my travels have I been to such a sports-crazy metropolis as Pittsburgh, and never have I been to such a mecca for pro athletes and their admirers as Froggy's. When owner Steve Morris bellows a gravel-voiced welcome to one of the legions of regulars, you understand why he is nicknamed Froggy.

And the regulars do troop into this convivial watering hole. The steady customers stop by for lunch when a big burger (the Bull Frog is the biggest), a Giant Club or Ryen's Hen (grilled barbecued chicken breast) fit the bill. They come by in even greater numbers after work, happily dunking veggies into a Curry Dip, quaffing draft beer and swapping stories. They come for dinner or late supper after a game, when they can choose from half a dozen kinds of steak, Prime Rib or succulent Baby-Back Ribs with Tim's Mom's Sauce. Froggy's is also the rare restaurant in the Middle Atlantic States where it is possible to get good New England Chowder and great Smoked Bluefish.

Froggy's establishment takes up two mid-Victorian storefronts on what is called Pittsburgh's oldest block. It is believed that this was the site of Watson's Tavern, built in about 1795 both as a pub and as the new nation's first criminal court. Whatever stood on that exact spot was a casualty of the Great Fire of 1835, but it is known that the present buildings, which date from 1850, at various times housed an olive oil refinery, a warehouse and a distribution center for washing machine parts.

Today Froggy's has an eclectic, casual atmosphere with bare wood floors, brick walls and open-beam ceilings. The long bar was built for the Monongahela House in 1900. The dining room in the adjacent storefront is furnished with sturdy oak chairs and large tables with plenty of elbow room. A fleet of ceiling fans suspended from the exposed joists rotate lazily, all driven by one motor and run off a complicated pulley system. Every square inch of wall space is covered with posters, autographed photographs, framed Leroy Nieman prints, jerseys and other sports memorabilia.

As I nibbled my way through samples of the kitchen's interesting output, I listened to Froggy Morris drop the names of the athletes who have stopped by to rub elbows with their admirers. Elbow-rubbing is about all the fans are allowed to do, because customers who hassle the players aren't tolerated. The boss is the best enforcer of his own policy, because the burly Froggy Morris is a former University of Pittsburgh football player.

A player, yes; a star, not really. But Froggy has become a celebrity since he opened his place in 1974. When ABC's *Monday Night Football* broadcast live from the restaurant, three hundred people called on the phone with various questions and comments. Froggy owns a bus and a fire truck, suitably identified, to haul seventy or eighty customers to a Pirates, Steelers or Pitt game. Froggy Morris is definitely no low-profile character. And his restaurant is no place for introverts, seekers of solitude or people who don't give a fig about sports. But for the rest of us, what a neat place.—c.w.

Froggy's is located at 100 Market Street in Pittsburgh. The restaurant is open Monday through Saturday from 11:00 a.m. until 2:00 a.m., although the kitchen closes at midnight. It is also open on Sundays when the Steelers are playing. For reservations call (412) 471-FROG.

FROGGY'S LYONNAISE POTATOES

1½ pounds redskin potatoes, washed but unpeeled
½ stick butter or margarine
1 teaspoon garlic powder or finely minced fresh garlic
1 teaspoon celery salt
1 teaspoon paprika
pinch of white pepper
½ cup chopped onion

Bake potatoes at 425 degrees for about 25 minutes, or until tender, and let cool. Cut cooled potatoes into quarters and then slice crosswise into bite-sized pieces. Melt butter in a large skillet. Meanwhile, mix seasonings and set aside. Sauté onions until they begin to wilt. Add potato pieces and heat through, stirring gently. Stir in seasonings. Serve immediately. Serves 4 to 6.

FROGGY'S BABY-BACK RIBS WITH TIM'S MOM'S SAUCE

1 cup soy sauce
1 cup yellow mustard
1¼ cup black molasses
⅓ cup Worcestershire sauce

¾ cup apple cider vinegar
cayenne pepper to taste (optional)
2 racks of baby-back ribs

Mix together the soy sauce, mustard, molasses, Worcestershire sauce, vinegar and cayenne pepper. Marinate ribs overnight in the sauce. Preheat oven to 250 degrees. Place ribs on rack and roast for 1½ to 2 hours, basting periodically and turning once, until meat is cooked through and tender. Or follow the same procedure and roast at extremely low temperature, 200 degrees, for four hours. Serves 8.

FROGGY'S CURRY DIP

2 cups mayonnaise
4 teaspoons curry powder
2 tablespoons Worcestershire sauce

¼ cup onion, minced very finely or puréed in a food processor

Stir all the ingredients together thoroughly and chill. Serve as a dip for fresh vegetables. Yields 2¼ cups.

CENTURY INN
Scenery Hill

CENTURY INN

From the glassed-in rear dining room of the Century Inn, it is possible on a clear day to see Pittsburgh, an hour's drive yet light years away. The view explains the quaint name of this hamlet along U.S. Route 40.

A rambling two-laner, Route 40 looks like a back road now, but it has been a key transportation link for centuries. As the Nemacolin Indian Trail, it was already an established route when young George Washington and his militia fought in the French and Indian wars. It was later widened and became the famous National Road, linking the Atlantic seaboard with the frontier. In 1794, Stephen Hill, who owned several stagecoach lines, built what is now the Century Inn as a stop between Washington and Brownsville, Pennsylvania. (In those days a stop was needed every twelve miles, which was the limit for a team of oxen.) Today, that inn is the oldest one continually operating on this historic route.

General Lafayette, the French marquis who played such a key role in the American Revolution, stopped at the inn for breakfast on May 25, 1825. Andrew Jackson was a guest twice before he became president—the second time on February 1, 1829, when he was on his way to Washington for his inauguration.

Dr. Gordon Harrington and his wife, Mary, purchased the inn in 1945 and began refurnishing it with suitable antiques. Their son Gordon and daughter-in-law Megin now run it. Megin and Mary hand-stenciled the plaster walls in the bar with patterns cut from the tracings of Moses Eaton, one of the few recognized stencilers of the early 1800s.

There are five dining rooms and each one is more inviting than the last. My companion and I dined in the Keeping Room, which had been the kitchen until 1956. Its fireplace is built of huge blocks of limestone quarried on the property. The many antiques, the flowered tablecloths topped by straw mats and the subdued lighting give the room a suitable country feeling.

In this era of *nouvelle cuisine*, New American fare and experimental cookery, the Century Inn is an unabashed outpost of

198

traditional American food. Megin says she has experimented with French dishes offered as specials, but they simply didn't sell. People come to this historic restaurant for the dinners they remember from Grandmother's house, or to eat as they imagine people did in the eighteenth century.

I had Country Pâté as an appetizer and Roast Turkey as an entrée. My dinner plate arrived heaped with moist white and dark meat, well-seasoned bread stuffing, Cranberry Sauce and an old-fashioned side dish of Bean and Ham Savory. My companion ordered "the usual," the Stuffed Pork Chop, which she says is so good that she never has anything else on her frequent visits.

The next time I'm in the neighborhood, I plan to stay in one of the seven second-floor guest rooms filled with antiques, country prints and charm. There is also a suite and an eighth bedroom, but the latter, called the Dolly Madison Room, is reserved for the Harringtons' collection of dolls and other toys from yesteryear.—c.w.

The Century Inn is located along Route 40 in Scenery Hill. Lunch is served from noon until 3:00 p.m., Monday through Saturday. Dinner is served from 4:30 p.m. until 7:30 p.m., Sunday through Thursday, and from 4:30 p.m. until 8:30 p.m., Friday and Saturday. Breakfast is served only to overnight guests. The inn is closed from just before Christmas through mid-March. For reservations (required) call (412) 945-6600.

CENTURY INN'S CHICKEN MARIAN

1 cup cornflake crumbs
4 slices of bacon, fried crisp and crumbled, reserving the drippings
2 tablespoons rich chicken stock

2 cups cubed cooked chicken
Cheese Sauce (recipe below)

Preheat oven to 375 degrees. Mix cornflake crumbs, bacon pieces, bacon drippings and stock. Spread half of this mixture in a 9x12x2-inch baking dish. Place chicken on top of the

199

crumb mixture. Pour Cheese Sauce over chicken, inserting a knife into ingredients in baking dish to allow the sauce to penetrate all the layers. Top with remaining crumb mixture. Bake for 35 to 40 minutes. Remove from oven and allow to rest for about 10 minutes before cutting into squares. Serves 8.

Cheese Sauce:

2 tablespoons butter or margarine
2 tablespoons flour
salt and white pepper to taste

1¼ cups milk
4 ounces sharp American or Cheddar cheese, shredded

In a skillet over low heat, melt butter or margarine. Whisk in flour, salt and pepper. Add milk all at once and continue whisking to blend. Cook, whisking, until mixture thickens and bubbles. Stir in cheese and continue cooking and stirring until cheese melts.

CENTURY INN'S BEAN AND HAM SAVORY

20 ounces canned green beans, well drained, reserving the liquid
3 ounces canned pimiento, well drained and chopped
3 ounces canned water chestnuts, drained and sliced

1 tablespoon sweet butter
½ cup chopped onion
1 cup diced cooked ham
1 tablespoon rich chicken stock

In a saucepan, combine the beans, pimiento and water chestnuts. Meanwhile, melt the butter in a skillet and sauté the onion and ham until the onion begins to wilt. Mix reserved liquid from the beans and the stock. Add liquid and onion-ham mixture to the vegetables. Simmer uncovered for 25 minutes, stirring occasionally. Serves 8 to 10.

INDEX

202

VEGETABLES